VOICE & VOTE

CELEBRATING 100 YEARS OF VOTES FOR WOMEN

Edited by Mari Takayanagi,
Melanie Unwin and Paul Seaward

THE HISTORY OF
PARLIAMENT
British Political, Social & Local History

SJH

VOTE100

Printed in England by Gavin Martin Colournet Limited on 150gsm Essential Silk. This paper has been independently certified according to the standards of the Forest Stewardship Council® (FSC)®.

A catalogue record of this publication is available from the British Library.

ISBN: 978-1-906670-70-2

Front cover and page 6
Nancy Astor, Viscountess Astor (1879–1964), campaigning during the 1919 by-election at Plymouth Sutton.
© Universal History Archive/UIG via Getty Images

CONTRIBUTORS

Paula Bartley has written historical biographies of Emmeline Pankhurst, Ellen Wilkinson and Queen Victoria and is presently writing a biography of women Labour Cabinet Ministers.

Elaine Chalus is Professor of British History at the University of Liverpool. She is particularly interested in the operation of gender and political culture prior to 1832.

Krista Cowman is Professor of History at the University of Lincoln. She has written widely on women's lives and women and politics in the late 19th and early 20th centuries.

Emma Crewe is Professor of Social Anthropology at SOAS, University of London, and is author of *House of Commons: an Anthropology of MPs at Work* (Bloomsbury, 2015).

Amy Galvin-Elliott is a PhD student jointly supervised by the History Department at the University of Warwick and the Parliamentary Archives. She is currently researching female experience of parliamentary spaces in the 19th century.

Oonagh Gay was head of the Parliament and Constitution Centre at the House of Commons Library, and has written widely on constitutional matters. She is a volunteer for the UK Parliament Vote 100 project, producing blogs and papers on early women MPs.

Elizabeth Hallam Smith, formerly Librarian at the House of Lords, is now a Leverhulme Trust Emeritus Research

Fellow based in Parliament, currently researching the history of St Stephen's Cloister and Undercroft.

Helen McCarthy is Reader in Modern British History at Queen Mary University of London and author of *Women of the World: The Rise of the Female Diplomat* (Bloomsbury, 2014).

Simon Morgan is Head of History at Leeds Beckett University, author of *A Victorian Woman's Place* (I.B. Tauris, 2007) and co-editor of *The Letters of Richard Cobden* (Oxford University Press, 2007–15).

Louise Raw is an independent historian, speaker and journalist. She is author of *Striking a Light: the Bryant & May Matchwomen and their Place in History* (Bloomsbury, 2011)

Sarah Richardson is Associate Professor of History at the University of Warwick and author of *The Political Worlds of Women: Gender, Politics and Culture in Nineteenth-Century Britain* (Palgrave, 2013).

Kathryn Rix is Assistant Editor of the House of Commons 1832–1945 project at the History of Parliament Trust and has recently published *Parties, Agents and Electoral Culture in England, 1880–1910* (Boydell and Brewer/Royal Historical Society, 2016).

Jane Robinson is author of *Hearts and Minds: Suffragists, Suffragettes and How Women Won the Vote* (Doubleday, 2018).

Paul Seaward is British Academy / Wolfson Research Professor at the History of Parliament Trust. He has written on the history of Parliament and on 17th-century politics and political thought.

Anne Stott is an independent researcher who has written on William Wilberforce and Hannah More. She is currently writing the life of Princess Charlotte, the daughter of the Prince Regent.

Duncan Sutherland came from Canada to study British parliamentary history at Cambridge University. He worked at the Centre for Advancement of Women in Politics at Queen's University Belfast and has also studied Singaporean and Jamaican history.

Mari Takayanagi is Senior Archivist at the Parliamentary Archives, and a historian who works on Parliament and women in the early 20th century. She is the co-curator of "Voice and Vote: Women's Place in Parliament".

Jacqui Turner is Lecturer in Modern History at the University of Reading. Her current research interests concern Nancy Astor and early female MPs. She has recently written on religion and the labour movement and Conservative women.

Melanie Unwin is the Deputy Curator and Head of Interpretation for the Parliamentary Art Collection. She is the co-curator of "Voice and Vote: Women's Place in Parliament".

INTRODUCTION

The Representation of the People Act 1918 marked a crucial milestone in the struggle of women in the UK for the right to vote. The Act finally enabled a majority of women over 30 years old to vote in parliamentary elections. It had been more than half a century since the first attempt to get Parliament to change the law; over 50 years of brave, inventive and determined campaigning by both women and men at all social levels, through many setbacks and despite sometimes intense divisions over strategy and tactics. In the same year the Parliament (Qualification of Women) Act was also passed, ensuring that women were not only able to vote for Members of Parliament, but to become Members themselves.

This book, which accompanies a major exhibition in Westminster Hall to mark the 2018 suffrage and parliamentary equalities anniversaries, tells the story of women's involvement in politics and in Parliament, and of their struggle for equal representation. It deals with the often forgotten part women played in politics before the middle of the 19th century, and the pioneers of women's suffrage; with the long campaign for the vote, and with the experience and achievements of female parliamentarians since winning it.

The book, like the exhibition, is arranged around the spaces with which women were associated within Parliament: the Ventilator, in the attic above the House of Commons chamber before 1834, from where women, out of sight and out of mind, watched and analysed the proceedings; the "Cage", the nickname for the Ladies' Gallery, where women spectators were isolated safely hidden behind grilles in the new chamber after 1850; the "Tomb", the small "Lady Members' Room" prepared for the convenience of the women Members who arrived in the years after 1918; and the Chamber, marking the final arrival of women in the late 20th century in the very highest offices of state, and presiding over proceedings in the Speaker's Chair in the House of Commons, and the Woolsack in the House of Lords.

The two 1918 Acts were not the culmination of women's struggle, for it would be another 10 years before women's voting rights were made equal to men's; it took four decades before women were able to become members of the House of Lords; and, although in the last 20 years many more women have been elected to the Commons, they still make up only a third of the House. Much more remains to be done, but this book records and celebrates what has been done: the huge achievement both of those who worked to achieve the representation of women, and of the women who have worked to represent the rights and interests of others.

CONTENTS

June 1854 ... Sketch of

THE VENTILATOR: BEFORE 1834

Before the later 19th century, women – unless they were monarchs – were excluded from virtually all formal positions of political power. However, this did not mean that they had no political views or played no part in public campaigns. Women were highly visible throughout political life – in elections, in campaigns, in the salons that operated in the background of politics, and as the staff who made parliament work. At times in the 18th century their presence in the chambers themselves was very conspicuous, as visitors in the galleries of both Houses. But after 1778, women were largely barred from the gallery in the Commons.

Elaine Chalus
Amy Galvin-Elliott
Elizabeth Hallam Smith
Sarah Richardson
Anne Stott

Previous pages
Sketch of Ventilator,
House of Commons, by
Frances Rickman, 1834.
The artist, a frequent
visitor to the Ventilator,
captures the architecture
of the space as well as
figures of women listening
to the debates below in
the Commons chamber

Above
"Roof of St Stephens,
Listening to the Debates
thro' the Ventilator", by
unknown artist, 1833

THE GALLERIES AND THE VENTILATOR

Instead, they had to watch proceedings from the obscurity, and heat, of the attic above the chamber, looking down at the Members' feet and the tops of their heads through a strange contraption designed to let out air, the ventilator. The move resulted from the efforts of several Members to exclude the public from the House in order to prevent the newspapers from reporting Parliament's proceedings, and came after an incident in which the Speaker had attempted to clear the gallery, but female observers had resisted. *The Times* described the resulting fracas as "a state of most extraordinary ferment and commotion" as "officers found their duty of turning out the fair intruders no easy work; a violent and determined resistance was offered to them." Afterwards men were able to return to the galleries, but women were not, as "the good sense of the country was opposed to making the ladies of England into political partisans." Unable to view the debates in the conventional way, women discovered the space of the ventilator.

The 18th century House of Commons chamber was the medieval St Stephen's Chapel, part of the old Palace of Westminster. In the 17th century a false ceiling had been built, to cover the high vault. A chandelier hung from the ceiling, and above it a ventilation shaft was built to take heat and fetid air from the chamber. It also

provided a view of the feet and the tops of the heads of the leading politicians below. Conditions were less than ideal: there was only enough space for a small number of people (one source says 14), and it was hot and uncomfortable. Nevertheless, the ventilator became a popular space for women to engage with politics. Not much is known about how it was used. The little evidence we have – from private letters – suggests that the spectators present were largely middle and upper class, though maids and attendants were also there, and others may have been present. As it was not an officially recognised parliamentary space, there is an absence of official records as to who was present. Presumably it was used until the fire of 1834 destroyed the original House of Commons chamber.

The Lords had been even more reluctant than had the Commons to allow visitors into its chamber, though as with the Commons, the presence of non-Members was often connived at. The peers decided to build a gallery (for the use of its Members) in 1704, but removed it in 1711. After another quarter of a century they decided to reinstate it; but in 1739 an incident foreshadowing that in the Commons nearly 40 years later may have encouraged them to take it down again. An attempt to keep spectators out of the gallery met spirited resistance from a group of highly-placed women including the Duchess of Queensberry. The House

Right
The Ventilator,
House of Commons,
by Lady Georgiana
Chatterton, 1821

Below
View of the Interior of the
House of Commons during
the Sessions 1821–23, by
James Scott, 1836. Above
the chandelier is the grille
that covered the Ventilator

Above

The Westminster Election,
1796, by Robert Dighton.
Women of all classes are
present in the crowd

only brought galleries back when it had moved to a
larger chamber, and when it needed additional space
for the "trial" of Queen Caroline in 1820. At first this
was a temporary structure; only in 1831 did it finally
decide to create a proper gallery, when a small part of
the gallery was made available for women – ironically
only a few years before the chamber was destroyed
in the fire of 1834.

WOMEN AND ELECTIONS

While women were not directly involved in the debates
in Parliament they were, therefore, very much a
presence at Westminster. And similarly, while women
may not have been able to vote, they were far from
absent from electoral politics. An election campaign
in pre-reform Britain was a celebratory, ritual and
often disorderly occasion in which voters and non-
voters – men, women and children – were involved.
They carried banners, marched in processions, lined
the streets and gathered in the windows, expressing
their allegiance to one or other candidate physically,
visually and vocally. The presence and approval of that
"more delightful portion of the creation" was frequently
commented upon by contemporary reporters. But it
would be vastly underplaying women's electoral
involvement if we assumed that it stopped – at any

level of society – at providing incidental colour or
political window dressing.

Women in the late 17th and 18th centuries
participated in election processions and treats; they
sewed banners and made cockades; they served
copious amounts of bread, cheese, beer and cider to
voters and non-voters alike (some of which was likely
to have been produced by women); and they capitalised
on the influx of business that the election brought to
their taverns and lodging-houses. Voters' wives were
also often more directly involved, especially during
contested elections. They were frequently canvassed
by candidates and their agents, as they were presumed
to have – and often did have – influence over their
husbands' votes. Coaxed, cajoled and oft-times kissed,
they might also be offered small amounts of cash or
douceurs. Offers of drink, dresses (possibly in the
candidate's colours) and the payment of debts were not
uncommon; neither were hints of (or threats to) future
patronage. While some women were flattered, persuaded
or cowed into agreement, others took open pleasure
in resisting all blandishments, proudly proclaiming their
personal or familial political independence. Lady Susan
Keck, canvassing on behalf of one of the candidates in
the 1754 Oxfordshire election, grumbled at being
obstructed by just such a "Viper", who "told me she

Above

"Canvassing for votes:
Plate II (Four Prints of
an Election)", by William
Hogarth, 1757. One of four
prints produced by Hogarth
as a criticism of election
corruption. The presence
of women suggests they
were active players in
the process

always was of the high party", whereas Lord Townshend, canvassing in Tamworth in 1765, noted several such wives ruefully in his notebook: "Wife governs, against us"; and then again, "wished us well, but his wife governed". The most formidable of voters' wives might even use the election to settle old personal scores with the local men who canvassed, or pointedly make formal complaints of bribery and corruption against canvassers whom they felt had been disrespectful.

Local women could also be part of the country's formal election machinery. Women, especially older women, can be found serving as witnesses during the process of the election, drawing upon their personal knowledge of people and places to challenge or confirm individuals' rights to vote. Sometimes they accompanied "tallies" – groups of voters – to the hustings to oversee the process of voting. When the result of an election was disputed, and the case was argued out in Parliament, women who often are otherwise completely missing from the historical record – female servants, tavern-keepers, laundresses, chimney sweeps' wives, and the like – joined local men, at candidates' expense, to testify. Ironically, the depositions of these women, who did not vote themselves, served to shape parliamentary decisions and determine election outcomes.

For the women of the political elite, participation in electoral politics varied according to personal circumstances, individual character and commitment, but was generally an extension of the family's larger involvement in the local community. Politics was a family business and some degree of women's involvement was largely accepted and even expected by contemporaries. It could even be demanded by male family members. Their activities became problematic only when they appeared to cross class boundaries, particularly between elite women and working men (such as when the duchess of Devonshire was alleged to have kissed a butcher during the 1784 Westminster election), or when the women proved to be such charismatic political figures or successful canvassers that they emerged as political figures in their own right and implicitly challenged the established gender order, as Lady Susan Keck did in the Oxfordshire election of 1754.

Whether men or women, 18th-century electoral politics was not for the faint-hearted. The most successful female campaigners needed to be thick-skinned and self-confident, able to shrug off sexual slander and crass satire. Lady Susan Keck (a daughter of the duke of Hamilton and a former lady of the bedchamber to George II's daughters) was ideally suited to the fray: she combined quick wit, a forthright tongue, a ready pen and a well-developed sense of the absurd with hard-headed political pragmatism. Despite declining health, she relished the challenge of the election and was so actively involved in treating, organising and canvassing in support of the ultimately victorious side in the Oxfordshire election of 1754 that she became the target of many execrable ballads and satires. Criticised by the opposition's hacks for

Below
"Wit's last stake or The Cobling Voters and
Abject Canvassers", by Thomas Rowlandson,
1784. Georgiana Cavendish, Duchess of
Devonshire, is shown canvassing with
Charles Fox in the 1784 election, ostensibly
paying the cobbler's wife for her shoe repair,
but suggesting bribery, as well as indicating
the cobbler's wife may have influence over
her husband's vote

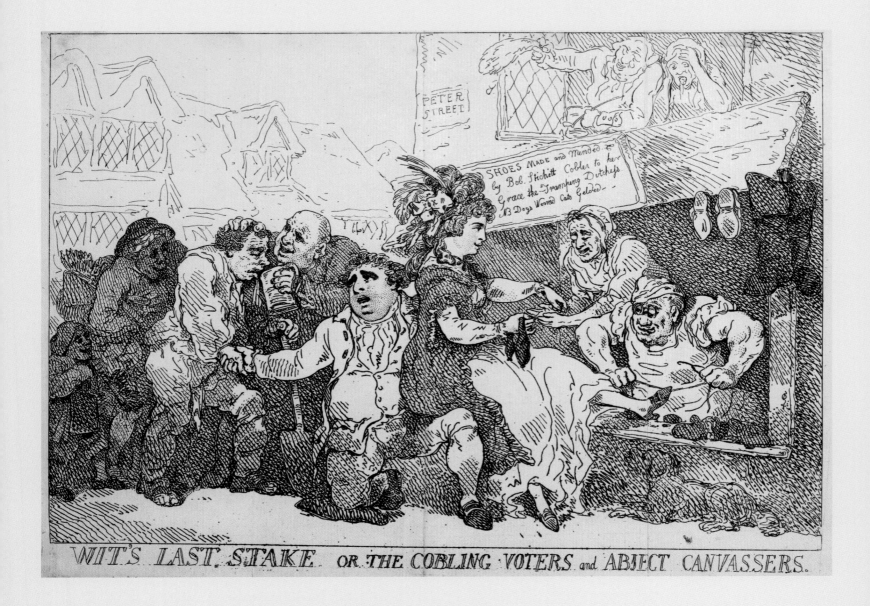

The Belle alliance, or the Female Reformers of Blackburn !!!

Above

"The Belle-Alliance or
the Female Reformers of
Blackburn!!!", by George
Cruikshank, 1819. Based on
an actual Reform meeting,
the print satirises the
Committee of the Female
Reform Society, who had
spoken from the platform,
as French revolutionaries

her looks, her hair, and her age, the gusto with which she embraced canvassing led her to be accused of unsexing herself – of becoming "my Lord Lady Sue". Adeptly, and with humour, she and the hacks on her own side neatly turned the argument on its head, undermining the masculinity of the opposition by pointing out that Lady Susan, while a woman, was the best "man" for the job. Her primary goal in the election was to energise the electors and to get out the vote – and she did both successfully.

What neither Lady Susan nor other 18th-century women did, however, was vote. While there are a couple of known cases of women voting in parliamentary elections in the 17th century, and a ruling in the courts in 1739 confirmed that women could vote for and hold minor parish offices, there is no evidence that women voted in parliamentary elections in the 18th century. That said, variations in the franchise and in customary practice meant that there were always some women who had recognised electoral privileges. Women had, in theory anyway, a legitimate interest in elections in around two thirds of all boroughs before the Great Reform Act of 1832. In some towns where the right to vote lay in the freemen, widows or daughters of freemen frequently had the right to make their husbands into voters. In others, the franchise was linked to the ownership of specific properties (burgages), and women who were the owners of burgages were at least technically entitled to vote until 1832. In Horsham in Sussex, for example, more than a fifth of the burgages were held by women in 1764. By custom their husbands would exercise the right to vote on their behalf; single and widowed women holding burgages would appoint proxies to exercise their votes. Many of these were undoubtedly male relatives, but the avidity with which these women were canvassed during hotly contested

elections (and burgage boroughs often saw repeated contests), and the amounts of money that women might be offered for their proxies or their property, shows their electoral importance.

Many elite families used the ownership of burgages to establish or secure their political control over, or at least some influence, or "interest", in the constituency. Lady Andover included her burgages and control over one seat at Castle Rising in her daughter's dowry. Lady Irwin, who inherited control over both seats at Horsham on her husband's death, fought repeated elections against the duke of Norfolk between 1778 and 1807. She managed to retain control of the borough and bequeath it and her political interest to her daughter. Other elite women managed burgage boroughs for absent husbands or underage sons. Even Sir James Lowther, a notorious "boroughmonger" – someone who collected boroughs for their own aggrandisement – owed a debt to his widowed mother Katherine, who purchased twenty-seven burgages in Appleby between 1751 and 1754, while he was still a minor, in order to ensure that the family retained control of one of the two seats. She similarly battled with Lord Egremont to buy up burgages in the borough of Cockermouth in 1756.

The importance of politically active widows controlling family interests should not be underestimated. Aristocratic families often experienced periods when the head of the family inherited when not old enough to take control of his own financial and political interests. It was common for the wife of the deceased to take over their management. The women who did so operated in much the same way as their male counterparts. They worked together with stewards and committees to plan strategy and canvassing, used tenancies to their electoral advantage and directed votes. They held "treats" for

Above
Above
Elizabeth Coke of
Derbyshire (1676–1739),
by Mary Beale, c.1690.
Coke was political agent
for her brother Thomas in
Grampound, Derbyshire,
in 1710

freeholders, flattered local gentry with entertainments
and public days and canvassed their peers in person
and by letter. They drew upon their female as well as
their male networks to achieve results.

There was always therefore a small group of
women who managed or controlled seats in Parliament
and whose political influence was recognised in the
locality and by the politicians managing elections in
London. The Dowager Lady Orford's control of both
seats at Callington and one seat at Ashburton was noted
in the 1750s and 1760s, as was Harriot Pitt's control of
one seat at Pontefract between 1756 and her death in
1763. There were other women, such as Lady Downing
who battled unsuccessfully for control of Dunwich in
Suffolk between 1764 and her death in 1778, who were
known political figures at the time but are less well
remembered now. The same is true of the many women
and men who possessed sufficient estates to give them
some local political significance, even if it did not go so
far as control of a whole borough.

Records of election campaigns underline how
for the elite at the time politics was a family affair.
Sisters, mothers, wives and widows might step in as
family representatives to cover for absent, ineffective
or underage men, or work in conjunction with male
family members to run election committees, organise
canvassers and direct campaigns. Elizabeth Coke,
seemingly out of frustration, took over her absent
brother's ill-organised campaign for Derbyshire in 1710.
She led the committee, planned strategy, oversaw
canvassing, tracked votes and used her social skills to
try and win over neighbours who had been annoyed
by her brother's politics, and wrote to chide him on his
non-appearance in the borough. After the election, she
stepped back seamlessly into her family role. Georgiana,
Countess Spencer, similarly managed elections at
St Albans for decades for her husband and son, while
they were preoccupied with campaigns in other family
boroughs. Despite being a political woman to her
fingertips, she exemplified the tensions some women
felt in electioneering. While she often grumbled about
politics, she embraced campaigning and clearly enjoyed
planning strategy and directing canvassing with her
committee. She remained very concerned, however,
about protecting her reputation and preserving her
physical and social distance from the electorate itself.
When canvassing in Northampton in 1774 along with
the candidate's wife, she spoke to voters from the safe
refuge of her carriage, putting "a little spirit into our
people" – which was the reason that her husband
had advised her to go – while also ensuring that they
did not threaten the social divide or their reputations.
Her daughters, Georgiana, Duchess of Devonshire,
and Henrietta, Countess of Bessborough, took a very
different tack ten years later in the vituperative 1784
Westminster election. As the most high-profile and
arguably most successful of at least 25 women who

"I have been in the midst of action – I have seen parties rise and fall"

Georgiana, Duchess of Devonshire

Left
Georgiana, Duchess of
Devonshire (1757–1806) by
Francesco Bartolozzi, after
Lady Diana Beauclerk (née
Spencer), 1779. As an elite
woman, Georgiana Duchess
of Devonshire had the
opportunity to see politics
from the inside

traditions and expectations, and specific election circumstances. The biggest changes after the Reform Act of 1832 would come for the women of the middle classes. It is they who would begin to attend political meetings; they who would sign anti-Corn Law petitions in the tens of thousands; and they whose teas and bazaars would defray the costs of voter registration and election expenses.

CAMPAIGNING WOMEN

Women's direct involvement in campaigning politics of this kind was not new in the early 19th century. Women were often at the forefront of protests in the 17th and 18th centuries, especially food riots, such as the raid near Oxford in 1766 during which sacks of flour were seized from a mill and distributed free. A common and established – almost ritual – form of protest, the food riot went beyond mere criminality. Women's prominence in them is easy to understand: they were the ones who suffered most if prices rose or grain was hoarded, and the legal position of married women could mean that it was their husbands, not they, who were held responsible for their actions.

From the Civil War of the mid-17th century we can see women participating more directly in the political arena. In February 1642, in the tense lead-up to the war, a group of women petitioning Parliament made the bold claim that because they were "sharers in the common calamities that accompany both church and commonwealth", they too had a role in public life. In August 1643, a year into the war, women launched their great peace petition. Hundreds wearing white silk ribbons in their hats massed outside the doors of Parliament calling for peace and the return of the King to London. They blockaded the House of Lords, and when soldiers turned up to disperse them, they tore their colours out of their hats. After two noisy hours, they were finally dispersed by a troop of horses.

The collapse of many of the institutions of the government and the church during the Civil War gave women new means of expression. Many were active in the separatist Protestant congregations that thrived as the authority of the established church fell away.

canvassed in this election, they became notorious for canvassing tradesmen on foot. The duchess was attacked in the press for exchanging kisses for votes in an attempt to drive them from the campaign with a barrage of sexual slurs. It almost worked.

Women did not retreat quietly into the confines of the domestic sphere as a result of either the nastiness of the 1784 election or concerns about gender and politics that were encouraged by the French Revolution. The Reform Act of 1832 made women's exclusion from elections explicit by defining voters as "male persons", and women lost their only remaining electoral privileges with municipal corporation reform in 1835. But they did not lose their personal influence or their involvement in local elections. Moreover, they were not immune to Radical politics and would come to play an increasingly visible part in the campaigning movements from the 1790s onwards. At the top of society, elite women's electoral involvement remained largely unchanged. It continued to be based upon factors including character, ability and experience, strength of political beliefs, family

Some of them even preached in public, though this was widely condemned. The loosening of press censorship during the war meant that women found it possible to write and publish about controversial religious matters. One woman, Katherine Chidley, moved from religious polemics to political activism. During the 1620s she and her husband had been members of an illegal separatist congregation, or conventicle. Shortly after the Long Parliament met in November 1640, beginning the political crisis that would lead to Civil War, she published *The Justification of the Independent Churches of Christ*, a defence of congregational church government and wifely autonomy, in opposition to a book written by Thomas Edwards, a fierce opponent of the separatist congregations. In further pamphlets, she argued that the defence of separatism was "a task most befitting a woman", appealed for the release of imprisoned separatists and offered to debate with her opponents on church doctrine. In 1647, she and her son founded a separatist church in Bury St Edmunds.

Chidley's religious campaigning took her into politics, and the radical Leveller movement. She became prominent among female Levellers in London, and in April 1649, with hundreds of other Leveller women, she besieged Parliament demanding the release of their imprisoned leaders. When one of them, John Lilburne, was again on trial in 1653, she organised a petition to Parliament with, it was claimed, 6,000 signatures. When they delivered it, two MPs came out to tell them that "they being women and many of them wives... the Law took no notice of them". The women replied that they were not all wives and that those who were had husbands to protect them and to defend the liberties of the people. Nothing more is known about Chidley, who may have died shortly afterwards.

Chidley's turbulent career was made possible by the revolutionary times in which she lived. The reassertion of political and religious authority in the 1650s and afterwards again restricted the opportunities for women to involve themselves so directly in political campaigning. But the French Revolution a century and a half later, and the widespread enthusiasm for the religious and political freedom it engendered, encouraged more women to seek to make a contribution. The plea for liberty for religious dissenters was taken up at the end of the 18th century by the poet and educationalist, Anna Letitia Barbauld. In *An Address to the Opposers of the Repeal of the Corporation and Test Acts*, written in 1790, she attacked the Church of England and claimed full civil and political rights for religious dissenters, who were barred from holding civil office. The tract was written during the early phase of the French Revolution, in the wake of the fall of the Bastille and the Declaration of the Rights of Man, and she believed she was witnessing the dawning of a new and better age, a time of equality, rationality, and peace. This millenarian optimism was echoed later in the year in Mary Wollstonecraft's *Vindication of the Rights of Men*, a spirited riposte to Edmund Burke's deeply conservative *Reflections on the Revolution in France*. Like Barbauld she saw the Revolution as "a glorious chance... now given to human nature of attaining... happiness and virtue".

In 1792 Wollstonecraft took female campaigning to a new level when she produced her most famous work, *A Vindication of the Rights of Woman*. This was a hugely ambitious call for a radical restructuring of the relationship of the sexes, nothing less than "a revolution in female manners" so that women could "labour by reforming themselves to reform the world". Her "wild wish" was "to see the distinction of sex confounded in

Opposite and above
Petition from the inhabitants of Manchester in support of the Foreign Slave Trade Abolition Bill, 1806. This anti-slave trade petition is more than 5 metres long and includes more than 2,000 names, including some women

society", as "it is vain to expect virtue [she meant intellectual and moral qualities] from women till they are, in some degree, independent of men". Though she made a plea for women to have "a direct share… in the deliberations of government", this was not the main thrust of her argument. Instead she focused on the skills they might acquire and the professions that should be open to them if society were more rationally organised. Women might "study the art of healing and be physicians as well as nurses". They could study politics through wide reading. "Businesses of various kinds they might likewise pursue." Through hard work and independence women could become worthy of a public role. Despising the empty courtesies and flatteries offered them by men, they should rise "with the calm dignity of reason above opinion" and dare "to be proud of the privileges inherent in man". These novel arguments met with a predictable backlash. Horace Walpole spoke for many when he called Wollstonecraft "a hyena in petticoats".

Barbauld and Wollstonecraft were not the only campaigning women in the troubled 1790s. Anti-revolutionary women also entered the political debate. Hannah More's *Village Politics*, completed at the end of 1792, was a skilful distillation of Burke's counter-revolutionary arguments for a popular readership. The plight of the French émigrés, the refugees from the revolution, opened up another avenue for female campaigning. In 1793 a Ladies' Society was set up to raise subscriptions for the émigré clergy and Hannah More and the novelist Fanny Burney, who had married an émigré, published fund-raising pamphlets. Short-lived though it was, the campaign introduced many women to the previously masculine tasks of fund-raising and committee work.

Above all it was the cause of anti-slavery that drew women into campaigns. In 1787 the all-male Committee for the Abolition of the Slave Trade had been set up, and the following year saw a flood of abolitionist literature, much of it written by women.

to coincide with the opening of the parliamentary debate. The campaign's most famous member, William Wilberforce, was drawn into it partly through his friend, the Prime Minister, William Pitt, but also through Margaret Middleton, the wife of the MP and naval officer Sir Charles Middleton, whose home at Teston, Kent, became a centre for the abolitionist cause. Lady Middleton's friend, Hannah More, contributed a poem, "Slavery", to the cause, while the radical Helen Maria Williams argued for abolition in her *Letters on the French Revolution*. In 1791 Barbauld published her poem, "A Letter to William Wilberforce". If writing was one campaigning method open to women, the consumer boycott was another, and was particularly suited to their roles as purchasers and homemakers. From 1792 some women were refusing to buy West Indian sugar, and when sugar from the East Indies later became available they bought that instead. The abolitionist campaign crossed religious and political barriers, bringing together Anglicans and Dissenters, radical and conservative women. Many women joined in the petitioning campaign against the slave trade: several women, for example, can be identified among the more than 2,000 people from Manchester who signed a petition against the trade presented to the House of Lords in 1806.

After a campaign lasting 20 years, the slave trade was abolished in 1807 and, for a while, the abolitionists believed that slavery itself would die a natural death. When this hope proved illusory the Anti-Slavery Society was set up in 1823. Cautious emancipators like Wilberforce soon found themselves outflanked by radical women campaigners. In 1825 the first Ladies' Anti-Slavery Society was set up at the home of Lucy Townsend, the wife of a Birmingham clergyman. A network of other ladies' anti-slavery societies followed, which set up nationwide committees, collected subscriptions from women, and arranged quarterly meetings. One of the most innovative and persistent of the campaigners was the Quaker Elizabeth Heyrick,

leader of the Leicester Ladies' Anti-Slavery Society. She had already taken on the male establishment in 1824 when she published anonymously her pamphlet, *Immediate, not Gradual Abolition*, an argument she developed in two succeeding pamphlets. She was the first white British campaigner to voice the argument that black slaves were already making – that they were not prepared to wait for gradual emancipation or the slow amelioration of their condition. Her call was taken up by other ladies' societies until in 1831 her stance was finally adopted by the national Anti-Slavery Society. A woman campaigner, backed by a network of thousands of other women throughout the country, had brought about a major change in policy.

Contributions to the growing readership of newspapers, magazines and cheap pamphlets and books was an obvious means by which women, denied the opportunity for office, could intervene in public debate. In this way Harriet Martineau – historian, journalist, and social commentator – became one of the most noted intellectuals of the 19th century. Her fame, and particular attitude to the existence of God, caused a contemporary to quip, "There is no god, and Harriet Martineau is his prophet." Born in 1802 into a family of Unitarian manufacturers in Norwich, Martineau was forced by the failure of her father's business to earn her own living. Her breakthrough came in 1831 when she began work on *Illustrations of Political Economy*, a series of stories published monthly from February 1832, written to explain the principles of the free-market capitalism espoused by Thomas Malthus and James Mill. The tales gave her an entrée into London intellectual circles, where the ear trumpet she carried with her to counter her deafness made her an instantly recognisable figure. Between 1852 and 1866 Martineau contributed more than 1600 articles and leaders to the liberal *Daily News*. She espoused three causes in particular: anti-slavery, feminism, and the positivist movement in philosophy. The common thread running through them all was

"Women, like men, can obtain whatever they show themselves fit for"

Harriet Martineau

her belief in self-improvement. On her tour of the United States between 1834 and 1836 and in her *Society in America*, published in 1837, she expressed her "horror and loathing" of slavery, but also argued that true emancipation must come from the slaves themselves. The true heroes of anti-slavery, she believed, were the runaway slaves rather than the white abolitionists. The same principle applied to women. She believed that they must work for their emancipation: they should earn the franchise by becoming intelligent and responsible citizens – a position very close to Wollstonecraft's.

Martineau's actions and writings were dominated by her twin passions for justice and self-improvement, and much the same could be said of other women campaigners between the 17th and 19th centuries. Though most would not have thought of themselves as feminists, they made bold claims for women. Denied the right to vote or to sit in Parliament, they refused to stay silent. Through their polemical writings, consumer campaigns, fund-raising, and committee-work, they asserted their rights to be citizens and sharers in the public realm along with men.

WOMEN IN POLITICS

Women were often subjects of political debate – as well as being subject to the laws of the land generally, Parliament regularly legislated on matters relating to women. They were frequently petitioners, both as part of a group and often as individuals. They could be called in to give evidence to either House, particularly when they were involved in private Acts on subjects such as naturalisation, changes of name and estates: the earliest naturalisation Act held in Parliament is for a woman. Women were of course involved in divorces, which could only be completely achieved by obtaining a special Act of Parliament until the law was changed in 1857. Most divorces were procured by men, but in 1801, Jane Campbell successfully brought the first divorce Act obtained by a woman, on grounds of her

husband Edward Addison's "incestuous adultery" with her sister Jessy. Women were, of course, barred from participating directly in parliamentary debates in the chambers of the House of Commons and the House of Lords. But in the late 18th and early 19th centuries a great deal of parliamentary politics took place outside parliament: in the masculine world of committee rooms and political clubs that proliferated in the vicinity of St James's; but also in the female-managed arenas of drawing rooms, salons, dinners and garden parties. The "social queens", or political hostesses, who presided over them played a significant part in the political life of the nation.

By the early 19th century, as politics was slowly becoming less aristocratic and marginally more socially inclusive, a wide variety of political salons, "at homes", dinners and parties dominated the social landscape. They included the exclusive "pink" parties of the leading aristocratic hostesses such as Lady Londonderry or the Duchess of Devonshire; the intellectual and literary "blue" gatherings which were descended from the famous bluestocking salons of Elizabeth Montagu, Hannah More, Elizabeth Carter and Hester Piozzi from the 1760s; and the more modest provincial social evenings of the urban middle class which were important in shaping civic political culture. In an era before formal party organisation, political salons, assemblies and soirées, and their enduring popularity were arenas for developing networks, bestowing patronage, and sharing news. The very informality of political life created spaces where women with the right connections and political motivations could thrive. These were mixed-sex, often cross-class, groupings where the female organisers could seek to influence the fortunes of governments, make or break the career of an aspiring politician, shape ministerial policies, and determine the outcome of elections.

The most influential and famed political hostesses were the aristocratic women who played a key role in managing party politics in the last quarter of the 18th

Above

Addison/Campbell Divorce
Act and associated
papers, 1801

century and the first quarter of the 19th. The Duchesses of Gordon, Sutherland and Devonshire and Ladies Palmerston, Holland, Waldegrave and Jersey were amongst the most prominent. Many of these women became politicians in their own right, rather than just supporters of their husbands' interests. After Georgiana, Duchess of Devonshire, had been publicly shamed for openly canvassing for votes for Charles James Fox in the 1784 Westminster election, she transferred her energies to nurturing alliances behind the scenes and was a significant player in the formation of the "Ministry of all the Talents" coalition in 1806. Not all political hostesses acted independently from their husbands: many male politicians owed their success to the efforts of their wives. Elizabeth Lamb used her dinners and parties to raise the profile of her husband, Lord

Melbourne, the future Prime Minister, who was created a peer in 1770 and promoted to a Viscount in 1781. She managed her husband's electoral interests in Bedford and worked hard to counter Melbourne's reputation as a philanderer and rake.

The Conservative premier Benjamin Disraeli, a regular attendee at the parties, soirées, dinners and salons of Mayfair, lampooned the figure of the political hostess in his novel *Endymion* (1880), basing his character Zenobia on the flamboyant society figure Lady Jersey, who acted as a key political confidante for the Whigs before changing sides and championing Wellington and Peel during the discussions on parliamentary reform in the 1830s. She was, he wrote: "the queen of London, of fashion, and of the Tory party... To be her invited guest under such circumstances proved at once that you had entered the highest circle of the social Paradise".

Social events in London usually took place in a town house close to Westminster. Lady Palmerston entertained at Carlton House Terrace and Cambridge House; Lady Waldegrave at Carlton Gardens; Lady Melbourne at Sackville Street and Piccadilly; and Lady Jersey at Berkeley Square. These were particularly important during the re-building of parliament after the fire of 1834. There were often two or three parties per evening and visitors would go from one to the next. The leading political hostesses would often confer so their parties did not clash. Such events played an important part in the lives of leading male politicians. George Canning during his first 16 months as an MP between 1793 and 1795 went to Mrs Crewe's suppers

and salons 47 times and Lady Payne's soirées ten times; he dined at Lady Charlotte Greville's nine times, Lady Malmesbury's 34 times and with the Countess of Sutherland 36 times.

A good deal of back-room politics took place at these social events. Patronage could be bestowed or removed, talented young politicians might find a safe parliamentary seat or a place in cabinet, alliances could be forged or dismantled and ministries could be formed. The "*salonnières*" often played a key role in smoothing political disputes by hosting parties attended by those of all shades of the political spectrum. Lady Stanley of Alderley, described by Palmerston as the co-whip (with her husband) of the Whig party, held a popular salon at her home in Dover Street. Realising his importance to the Whigs, she was the first aristocratic hostess to invite Daniel O'Connell, the

Left
Dinner at Haddo House, 1884, by Alfred Edward Emslie, 1884. The campaigner and philanthropist Ishbel Maria-Gordon, Countess of Aberdeen, presides over a dinner with the prime minister, William Gladstone, to her right, and the future prime minister, the Earl of Rosebery, to her left

Above
Trial of Queen Caroline in House of Lords 1820, by J. G. Murry, after James Stephanoff. Queen Caroline, the only woman present, is shown seated surrounded by male Peers and others

controversial leader of the Irish MPs, to her drawing room. She gave a banquet in his honour, followed by a reception for politicians to meet him. The evening was described as the most important social and political event of the season. Lady Palmerston also invited a broad spectrum of political opinion to her receptions. In 1852 following the collapse of Lord John Russell's Liberal ministry, over three hundred people attended including three members of Lord Derby's newly formed Conservative cabinet and over 40 backbench MPs.

These very public social occasions contrasted with the more intimate roles these powerful women could play. Harriett Arbuthnot for instance acted as a political sounding board for the senior Tory politicians Lord Castlereagh and the Duke of Wellington. Castlereagh visited her nearly every day at breakfast between 1820 and his suicide in 1822, in her words, "to take his orders". Later, Wellington forewarned her of every major initiative of the Tory ministries including George IV's divorce from Queen Caroline, Catholic Emancipation and Parliamentary reform. He showed her confidential letters from the King and foreign courts and often consulted with her before he referred matters to his cabinet. Harriett was thus soon regarded by politicians and foreign diplomats as the conduit for access to the highest echelons of the Tory administrations.

In the 19th century, the aristocracy's dominance over parliamentary politics began to be challenged by a new group of middle-class politicians. The established hostesses incorporated these men into their parties and suppers but new salons sprang up frequented by men and women who met on equal terms. These assemblies often had a more intellectual character than the traditional gatherings, with topics such as current affairs, art, philosophy, religion and literature regularly on the agenda. Political economy was an immensely fashionable topic in the so-called "blue" salons (to distinguish them from the aristocratic "pink" parties) of the early 19th century. Drawing rooms and dinner parties were buzzing with discussions on the currency question, the value of labour and the classical principles of political economy. The novelist Maria Edgeworth wrote in 1822 that: "It has now become high fashion with blue ladies to talk political economy. Meantime fine ladies now require that their daughters' governesses should teach political economy." Women such as Harriet Martineau and Jane Marcet regularly challenged politicians and economists at these gatherings, influencing the development of economic policy.

Although London continued to be the centre of such activities for aristocratic and middle-class hostesses, salons also developed in the towns and cities of the rapidly industrialising nation. Susannah Taylor held a regular influential gathering in Norwich during the French wars. It was here Harriet Martineau obtained her political education, joined by other women destined to play a significant part in early 19th-century politics, including Amelia Opie and Sarah Austin. The women of the Darwin-Wedgwood clan were also active in organising salons at their homes in London and the Midlands, and even abroad: Jessie Sismondi, sister-in-law to Elizabeth Wedgwood, held a regular "Thursday evening" party at her home in Geneva. These networks proved crucial for the circulation and exchange of news on domestic and foreign affairs.

THE DEMAND AT PETERLOO FOR
UNIVERSAL ADULT SUFFRAGE IN 1819!!!

THE DEMAND AT WESTMINSTER FOR
UNIVERSAL ADULT SUFFRAGE IN 1908???

ST STEPHEN'S CHAPEL & SPEAKER'S HOUSE.
from Westminster Bridge.

And beyond the world of salons and polite
networks, women were – as they always had been –
involved in organising, supporting in, and engaging in,
protest and radical politics, the great movement for
political reform in the early part of the 19th century
that would eventually result in the achievement of the
Reform Act of 1832. Women were present at the great
meeting in 1819 in Manchester that resulted in the
Peterloo massacre: many were injured and some died.
The campaigns for reform demanded the removal of
corruption and aristocratic influence in the constitution,
and the proper representation of newly industrialised
and urban areas; they did not encompass yet a demand
that women be given the right to vote. But women
were starting to use the arguments of reformers to
push for change, even if they could expect little serious
consideration. A petition was presented on 3 August
1832 from an individual, Mary Smith of Stanmore in
the County of Yorkshire, by the radical MP Henry Hunt,
who had been at the centre of the Peterloo rally in
1819. The petitioner stated that: "she paid taxes, and
therefore did not see why she should not have a share
in the election of a Representative; she also stated that
women were liable to all the punishments of the law, not
excepting death, and ought to have a voice in the making
of them." Her petition was laughed out of the House.

WOMEN WORKING IN PARLIAMENT

From the fruit sellers of Westminster Hall to the servants,
wives and children in grace and favour houses, women
were a constant if generally unobtrusive background
presence in the old Palace of Westminster. Before much
of the original Palace of Westminster was burnt down in
the devastating fire of 1834, beautiful gardens stretched
down to the Thames where today the Commons terrace

stands. In the mid-19th century Anne Rickman, the
Clerk Assistant's daughter, recalled playing there in her
youth with the children of the Teller of the Exchequer,
Samuel Wilde, trailing their hands into the water at high
tide from Mrs Wilde's drawing room window.

The lot of many of the women workers at
Westminster was altogether less idyllic. They emerge in
low-status jobs, alongside men, in remarkably detailed
inventories of maintenance work at the Palace. One such
was the anonymous woman paid 9d in 1644 for "keeping
clean the seats of the House of Commons", another, a
"necessary woman" who in 1725-6 was allocated almost
£6 for taking care of its stool rooms – the lavatories.
In the Lords, the Gentleman Usher of the Black Rod
employed a necessary woman, Mary Phillips, in 1761;
and a female Fire Maker, Sarah Matthews, in 1768. In the
1770s Martha Harrison received about £3 a year for
night work and emptying the privies of both Houses,
and Elizabeth Mills, hallkeeper, £2 2s for the more
supervisory role of opening and shutting doors for
workmen. A few women exercised trusted, responsible
and well-remunerated roles, essential to the running
and upkeep of the ancient and patched-up buildings and
to the functioning of parliamentary business. One was
Peternelle Vernatty, a wealthy gentlewoman, who
between 1717 and 1731 was paid more than £200 per
parliamentary session for "setting up, lighting, maintaining
and repairing the lamps in Westminster Hall and other
places for the accommodation of both Houses of
Parliament". She had inherited her lucrative business
from her father, descendant of swashbuckling Dutch
entrepreneurs and the holder of a patent for candle
lamps; on her death, her business passed to her husband.

Although women occupied a significant place in
the capital's commercial life at this time, Vernatty was

unusual in running her own business while married. More typical of women entrepreneurs was Deborah Reding, a widow who from 1708-29 continued her husband's scavenging and maintenance operations, including clearing rubbish, drains and gutters for Parliament and "looking after the flap at the King's Bridge to prevent the tide overflowing". Similarly, from 1706–24 widow Anne Brown ran her late husband's business as a slater, repairing the roofs of the records room, the Lord Chancellor's apartments and the "bog house", all near Westminster Hall.

The vast majority of Parliament's salaried posts, though, were occupied exclusively by men until the late 20th century. The housekeepers of the House of Commons and the House of Lords were however an exception. The Lords' housekeeper was a grand and significant appointment made by the Lord Chamberlain on the crown's behalf. Established in 1509 and by 1700 paid some £130 a year, the duties of the housekeeper were to ensure the safety and security of the House. Its perquisites included the right to occupy or to let several rooms near the Lords' chamber. From 1573 to 1690 a succession of male Wynyards held this role, but on the death of John Wynyard in 1690 his daughter Anne succeeded as Lords' Housekeeper, occupying the role jointly with her husband John Incledon. In 1705, they described their apartments as comprising four rooms, some in a ramshackle state, cellars, washhouses and a garden: a 1718 plan reveals that the housekeepers occupied a substantial suite near to the House of Lords, somewhat larger than the adjoining room occupied by the Lord Chancellor. Anne died in 1705, her burial plaque at St Margaret's Westminster conventionally describing her as "a woman of modesty, integrity, prudence and singular piety". Thereafter, the office of Lords Housekeeper was occupied by several women, initially the Incledons' female descendants. The last pre-fire holder of the position, Frances Brandish, was an absentee, delegating her job to others. On the night of 16 October 1834, her duties were being undertaken by Elizabeth Wright, mother-in-law of her deputy. She was a prime suspect in allowing the fire to rage unchecked through the Palace.

The duties of the House of Commons Housekeeper were altogether more workaday, as were its incumbents. Reporting to the Serjeant-at-Arms, the Housekeeper was responsible for looking after the Commons chamber and committee meetings. Established in 1660 for Thomas Hughes, and subsequently held by his daughter Anne from 1692 to 1703, the office's allowance of £10 was raised to £30 in 1697. Anne's son and successor Thomas Smith was in 1716 awarded the additional duties of keeping clean the "house of office" (again, the lavatories) for the Commons, supervising the pumping of water and the flushing and cleansing of the vaults where the effluent was stored, all for a daily fee of 12d. On Thomas's death in 1722 these unattractive duties were retained by his widow, Sarah Smith – although the principal Housekeeper role passed to Thomas Ward with a doubling of his salary to £60. Fortunately for Sarah, the "bog house" was located to the south-west of the House's lobby and well away from her room, seemingly in the attic storey above the chamber. From here, she was additionally required to supervise the ventilation system for the Commons, devised by the eccentric inventor Dr Theophilus Desaguliers. This never worked properly, not least because, as Desaguliers later recalled, Mrs Smith: "did all she could to defeat the operation of these machines", vehemently refusing to light the fires required to get the air circulating, as they made her room too hot.

After Sarah's death in 1741, other women, Anne Hollingshead and Anne Stephens, at times exercised Sarah's cleansing and attendance duties, but this time jointly with their husbands. By 1811, when John Bellamy and his wife Maria became deputy Housekeepers, this role was much expanded. It brought in £429 a year, John's father having established a lucrative catering business, Bellamy's, selling coffee, wine and his famous mutton pies to MPs. One of Parliament's most celebrated institutions, in the 1830s Bellamy's was supervised by "Jane", eternally-youthful, flirtatious, clad all in black, whose leading characteristic was, Charles Dickens tells us in a satirical Boz sketch, to show "a thorough contempt for the great majority of her visitors".

Below
The Destruction of the Houses of Lords
and Commons by Fire on the 16th Oct
1834, by William Heath, 1834. In 1834
a huge fire swept through the old Palace
of Westminster. Westminster Hall was
saved but the House of Commons and the
Ventilator were destroyed

MAKING THE CAGE, 1834–97

In 1834 most of the Houses of Parliament was destroyed in a great fire. The Commons' and Lords' chambers were burnt down, and the ventilator went along with them. It provided an opportunity to re-think accommodation for women, and a Select Committee considered the issue in 1835 in relation to the House of Commons. It was eventually agreed that a separate Ladies' Gallery should be constructed, set apart from the men at the north end of the House, and "screened in front by an open trellis work".

Simon Morgan
Louise Raw
Kathryn Rix
Jane Robinson

From the beginning, women using the new Ladies' Gallery complained of the defective ventilation that made the space hot, stuffy and smelly. It was too small and cramped, nearby facilities were limited, and its position high above the Speaker's Chair meant the angle to view debates was very steep. The metal grilles, placed over the windows to place women outside the chamber and to prevent men being able to see the women watching then, made it dark and very difficult to see. The campaigner Millicent Fawcett, who had to spend many hours watching debates on behalf of her blind MP husband, wrote: "One great discomfort of the grille was that the interstices of the heavy brasswork were not large enough to allow the victims who sat behind it to focus… it was like using a gigantic pair of spectacles which did not fit, and made the Ladies' Gallery a grand place for getting headaches." The grilles became both a physical and metaphorical symbol of women's exclusion from Parliament, and later a target of suffragette agitation.

WOMEN IN EARLY VICTORIAN PUBLIC LIFE

Industrialisation, the growth of towns and cities and the expansion of the newspaper press contributed to the rapid extension of the public sphere from the early 19th century. The reform of municipal government in 1835 prompted the development of new forms of civic pride, reflected in prestigious buildings such as town halls and corn exchanges, but also in the proliferation of voluntary and charitable organisations. On the face of it, this was a world from which women were excluded. Evangelical religious movements fostered the idea that women moved in a "separate sphere" to men. Women's moral and spiritual authority was idealised, but their physical and intellectual capabilities downplayed. Theoretically, at least, women tended to be restricted to the domestic sphere. The "public sphere" of work, politics and voluntary organisation was held to be the domain of men. In practice, the

division was hard to achieve for many. Working-class women often had no choice but to work, either in domestic service or in industries such as textiles, ceramics and some of the metal trades.

Even for middle-class women, however, the boundaries were never rigidly fixed, and many talented women were able to push well beyond them. Indeed, the social, economic and cultural changes of the era opened up a surprising range of opportunities for women to contribute to public life. Evangelicalism, while it helped to restrict women's participation in public life, also encouraged women to take an active role in their communities as dispensers of charity and spiritual succour. Many women would become resourceful and energetic organisers of efforts for the relief of the poor. In 1817, the Quaker Elizabeth Fry set up a prison visiting society at Newgate, initially to look after the spiritual and physical needs of female inmates. In 1858 Louisa Twining set up the Workhouse Visiting Society for a similar purpose. Both women turned individual philanthropic activities into national movements. By the 1860s, "ladies' committees" were ubiquitous in prisons, workhouses and hospitals. Initially resented by male governors, their work became accepted as extensions of women's domestic roles as household managers and providers of emotional and spiritual comfort. But increasingly women like Fry and Twining built on their knowledge and experience to claim influence in growing areas of public policy.

Other women who followed this route to recognition and influence included the journalist and author Harriet Martineau, whose fictionalised tracts established her as a populariser of political economy in the 1830s and 1840s; Mary Carpenter, who worked for the reform of juvenile delinquents; and, most famously, Florence Nightingale. Nightingale achieved fame as the "lady with the lamp", tending to the wounded during the Crimean War (1854-56), but it was her analytical mind and capacity for hard work that underpinned her

Right
The House of Commons
in 1858, by Joseph Nash.
The Ladies' Gallery is behind
the stone screen high above
the Speaker's Chair

Above
Prison reform campaigner
and Quaker minister
Elizabeth Fry (1780–1845),
by Samuel Drummond, 1815

achievements in promoting hospital reform and the establishment of professional nursing. Pioneers such as temperance lecturers Anne Carlile and Clara Lucas Balfour, or the black American anti-slavery campaigner Sarah Parker Remond (who was active in Britain), leveraged their expertise to open the public platform to women. In 1857, experience gained locally through workhouse visiting, charitable work, and the promotion of sanitary advice to the poor was given a national platform with the foundation of the National Association for the Promotion of Social Science. This organisation encouraged women's participation from the start, providing opportunities to give formal papers on subjects of national concern to influential audiences.

As well as expertise and "woman-power", women made a key contribution to civil society through fundraising to support voluntary organisations. Nineteenth-century voluntary organisations were primarily funded by annual subscription. This was essentially a masculine system: subscription lists were published to encourage the wealthier residents of the town to contribute according to their means, and those who subscribed most exercised a disproportionate influence on the committee. Women of independent means could subscribe, but were barred from executive committees. As a minority, they exercised little collective influence. However, the reverse was true in women's and children's hospitals, or the

so-called "Magdalen Asylums" aimed at reforming prostitutes. In these "feminine" institutions women made up the overwhelming majority of subscribers and established women's committees that were vital to their continued operation. As subscribers to medical institutions, they could also exercise a degree of influence by voting on the election of medical staff.

Women developed distinctively feminine modes of fundraising. Door-to-door card collections were pioneered by women's auxiliary missionary societies, established from the 1820s onwards, which provided vital financial support to Christian missions overseas and in the backstreets of Britain's teeming cities. However, the most distinctive method was the bazaar, or ladies' sale, ranging from small affairs in support of a local charity, to elaborate festivals taking place over several days. They allowed women to contribute financially to campaigns and institutions that were not necessarily feminine in character. Their effectiveness brought female organisers a degree of public respect and acknowledgement. One of the most spectacular was held at Covent Garden Theatre in May 1845, raising £25,000 for the formidable electoral machinery of the Anti-Corn Law League. The league, which campaigned to abolish tariffs on imported food, blamed the Corn Laws for the prevailing poverty of the time. Women's involvement in a controversial campaign of domestic reform was a new departure, albeit based on the

A Corner in the Ladies' Gallery

Hy.F.

"A grand place for getting headaches"

Millicent Fawcett

Opposite
"A Corner in the Ladies'
Gallery", by Harry Furniss,
1888, showing women
leaning forward to peer
through the grilles

Above

The Corn League Bazaar held at the Theatre Royal in Covent Garden, London

precedent of women's anti-slavery activity, and seen as an extension of their charitable work and of their interest in cheap provisions as household managers. In later years, several veterans of the women's movement credited involvement in the Anti-Corn Law League as a key moment in their political education.

s   All this activity gave women experience of organisation beyond the purely domestic, while the gendered nature of the public sphere and their usually subordinate place within it helped foster a sense of collective identity. Some translated this into a desire to improve women's position. An important moment came with the 1851 census, which revealed for the first time the true extent of women's economic activity, along with a marked imbalance in the numbers of women over men, challenging the notion that women's economic needs were looked after by male relatives. In 1854, Barbara Leigh Smith (later Bodichon) published her *Brief Summary... of the Most Important Laws of England Concerning Women*, showing in particular how married women were disadvantaged by the law. Along with Bessie Rayner Parkes, she founded the *English Woman's Journal* in 1857, which campaigned for women's higher education, access to professions such as medicine, and reform of the marriage laws. The journal was closely associated with the Society for Promoting the Employment of Women, while the Social Science Association provided an important platform for their ideas.

Women had some successes before 1870 in amending the grossly unequal marriage laws. After a long and personal campaign by the author Caroline

Norton, the Infant Custody Act of 1839 allowed children of separated parents under the age of seven to reside with their mothers (previously custody had automatically gone to the father). The Matrimonial Causes Act of 1857 made divorce slightly more affordable, and granted divorced women some control over their property. The marriage laws were further amended in 1870 to allow married women the right to their own earnings. Women also maintained a toehold in local politics. Although municipal and poor law reform eroded its political significance, female ratepayers were often allowed to vote at parish vestry meetings according to custom, and in 1851, there were 865 women serving as church officials in England and Wales. After the reform of the Poor Law in 1834 women ratepayers could still vote for poor law officials, but were excluded from sitting as Poor Law Guardians until 1870, though the slow progress of the reforms meant that a landowner like Anna Maria Tempest could be elected overseer of the poor for the parish of Ackworth as late as 1849.

Some women were propelled into a more direct involvement in national politics by the Contagious Diseases (CD) Acts of 1864 and 1866. These Acts, provoked by a political panic about the spread of venereal disease in the army and navy, introduced compulsory health checks for women suspected of prostitution in port and garrison towns. The checks included invasive internal examination by speculum; but, as men were not subject to checking as well, the exercise was futile. The Acts provoked fury by placing responsibility for the contagion on women, and by

Right
Caroline Norton (1807–77),
by Frank Stone

attempting to ensure a supply of "clean" prostitutes for soldiers and sailors. The emphasis on suspicion rather than proof meant that any woman could be harassed by police and forced to undergo the examination. Many of the women were vulnerable and had no idea of their legal rights. A determined repeal campaign was led by feminist campaigner Josephine Butler, who successfully overturned taboos against women speaking in public on matters relating to sex. Butler argued that the state was effectively supporting immorality and encouraging sexual exploitation of working-class girls by middle-class men, threatening the sanctity of the middle-class home. On the one hand the campaign reinforced the notion that women's interests were primarily domestic; but on the other, it challenged the claim that women's political interests were identical with those of men and showed

that political decisions in the "public" domain could have direct effects on the "private" sphere of the home. The laws were repealed in 1886.

Women therefore exercised a profound, if often indirect, influence on public life before 1867. There was no consistent route from philanthropy to feminism. Some prominent women, including Nightingale, later opposed women's enfranchisement; others, such as Norton, expressed no interest in the subject. However, the experience many gained working on committees for charitable purposes, setting up educational institutions or raising and managing funds provided compelling arguments for the opening of local elected positions to women in the succeeding decades, and provided an important springboard to the vote itself.

It appears from the Handbills issued by MR. CHILDERS
this morning, that
HE IS AFRAID TO MEET US,
And answer our questions on the Contagious Diseases Acts.

THEREFORE
Mrs. BUTLER
REQUESTS THE
WOMEN OF PONTEFRACT
TO MEET HER AT THE
LARGE ROOM, IN SOUTHGATE,
(USED BY MR. JOHNSON AS A SPINNING ROOM),
THIS EVENING AT SEVEN O'CLOCK.
MRS. BUTLER will shew that the Bill of which MR. CHILDERS
says he is now a supporter, while pretending to Repeal the "Contagious
Diseases Acts" is an extension of their principle to the whole country.
MRS. BUTLER will shew that MR. CHILDERS belongs to a
Government which has extended these Acts not only to this Country
but to the Colonies and Dependencies of the British Empire.
JOSEPHINE E. BUTLER, Hon. Sec. of the Ladies' National Association.

Above

Josephine Butler
addresses the women
of Pontefract, 1872

WORKING-CLASS WOMEN AND PROTEST

Industrialisation in the 19th century radically altered perceptions of female labour. Women had worked since records began but, in agrarian societies, they were more likely to do so in family groups or small workshops, and to be paid in kind rather than currency. As the population shifted to burgeoning towns and cities, many women sought work beyond the home. Victorian commentators predicted disaster. They variously opined that women's wages were too low and would drive them "onto the streets", or were too high and would lure them to vice via the gin palace and music hall. The term "working girl" became a euphemism for "prostitute". Drunkenness amongst men, high mortality rates among working-class children, even the degeneration of the British race were all laid at the door of the very women who had helped to make industrialisation possible. In reality, the separation of home and workplace made working women's lives exponentially harder as they struggled to balance work and family. Their low earnings, around half the average male wage even for identical work, were justified by the myth of the "family wage" of the male breadwinner, and made them easy to replace. A survey of lives of the London poor in 1882 noted of women engaging in dangerous work at minimal wages: "Why do not the women refuse? Because they would be discharged… The struggle for bread is too fierce for the fighters to shrink from any torture in its attainment". Women without union strike pay needed great courage – or desperation – to take action. If arrested, they could be sentenced to hard labour. If not defeated legally, they were often simply "hungered back" to work.

Despite this, female workers fought against exploitation. The first all-female union on record was formed by Leicester hand-spinners in 1788. It was 18,500 strong, and notably militant. Strikes amongst women cotton workers were recorded in 1808 and 1818: during the latter, strike-breakers were dunked under water-pumps. Male and female spinners fought side by side for equal pay in Glasgow in 1833 and both sexes united in the struggle for parliamentary reform in the same decade. The all-inclusive Grand National Consolidated Trades Union, established in 1833, had a considerable female membership and self-organised women's branches.

Women were active and influential too in the Chartist movement, and were in the forefront of local campaigns against the Poor Law, the much-resented system for workhouse-based poor relief introduced in 1834. Chartism's explicit list of demands insisted only on universal male suffrage, and many (though far from all) Chartists, were either dismissive of the idea that women should also receive the vote, or regarded it as an impractical goal. Nevertheless, from 1838 onwards, as Chartism became a powerful national movement, many female associations were formed, some of them (such as the Birmingham Female Political Union) growing to thousands of members, though most were small local bodies. They were largely viewed by the men of the movement as having a valuable, but subordinate part to play in the campaign; and many men regarded women's

Treasures Drawer III   324.30941

12228

TO THE HONOURABLE THE COMMONS OF THE UNITED KINGDOM OF GREAT BRITAIN AND IRELAND IN PARLIAMENT ASSEMBLED.

The Humble Petition of the undersigned,

Sheweth,

That the exclusion of freeholders, householders, and ratepayers, legally qualified in every respect but that of sex, from the power of voting in the election of Members of your Honourable House, by depriving a considerable portion of the property, the industry, and the intelligence of the country of all direct representation, is injurious both to the persons excluded, and to the community at large.

That women are competent, both by law and in fact, to carry on a business, to administer an estate, and to fill other positions, which, both by investing them with interests requiring political representation, and by affording tests of fitness, are usually considered to give a claim to the suffrage.

That the admission of such persons to the privilege of the Franchise would be a measure in harmony with the principles of our representative system, while its beneficial effects would not be attended by any possibility of dangerous political consequences.

Your Petitioners therefore humbly pray that your Honourable House will take such measures as to your wisdom may seem fit for granting the suffrage to unmarried women and widows on the same conditions on which it is, or may be, granted to men.

And your Petitioners will ever pray.

NAME.   ADDRESS.

0838171

Above

Petition circulated by the Women's Suffrage Petition Committee, 1866. This document marks the start of the organised mass suffrage movement in the UK

Above

John Stuart Mill (1806–73), philosopher and politician, by P A Rajon after G F Watts

factions. With the decline of Chartism, the British labour movement would effectively turn its back on women for the next three decades. In 1875, Henry Broadhurst of the Trades Union Congress declared that its aim should be to "bring about a condition… where wives and daughters (are) in their proper sphere at home, instead of being dragged into competition for livelihood against the great and strong men of the world". He was sceptical when middle-class women began to appear at the annual TUC Congress to voice the concerns of working women, announcing that he "doubted… the wisdom of sending women to these congresses. Under the influence of emotion they might vote for things they would regret in cooler moments". Even after the founding of the Social Democratic Federation (SDF) and the Independent Labour Party, female equality remained largely an issue for women alone. The SDF leader Ernest Belfort Bax, touted as the "philosopher of the movement", was an avowed misogynist, and the author of *The Fraud of Feminism* (1913). Not until 1888 would spontaneous industrial action by those excluded from the labour movement force it to pay serious attention to women as a force to be reckoned with.

THE CAMPAIGN FOR WOMEN'S SUFFRAGE, 1866–97

In June 1866, John Stuart Mill, Liberal MP for Westminster, presented the first mass women's suffrage petition to the House of Commons. Signed by 1,521 women, it originated from debate at the Kensington Society, a discussion group for women, and was organised by a small informal committee. The leading figures behind it included Barbara Leigh Smith Bodichon, Bessie Rayner Parkes, Emily Davies and Elizabeth Garrett (later Anderson). Davies and Garrett brought the petition to Westminster Hall, and Davies later told the story of hiding it under the stall of an old woman fruit seller while they waited for Mill. Their support of women's suffrage was part of their wider advocacy of women's rights, campaigning on issues such as married women's property rights and female education and employment. Helen Taylor, whose mother Harriet Taylor had married Mill in 1851, described the women's demand for the vote in 1866 as "the first humble beginnings of an agitation". The next three decades saw sustained organisation and lobbying of Parliament by women to promote their cause, laying important foundations for the women's suffrage campaign after 1897.

role as to evoke sympathy by playing the victims of a harsh and repressive system. Yet the women were key to the organisation of Chartism, especially at a local level: women participated in meetings, demonstrations, riots, and the petitioning that was at the heart of the movement. They also developed interests and an importance beyond the wider movement. The influential secretary of the London Female Democratic Association, Elizabeth Neesom, called in 1839 for women to "shake off that apathy and timidity which too generally pervades among our sex", and asserted the rights of women "as free women (or women determined to be free) to rule ourselves". In the case of Neesom, activism was channelled into campaigning for women's education. There were many other causes, particularly temperance, that were given a fair wind through the networks and initiation provided by Chartism.

Chartism peaked as a movement in the late 1830s. Thereafter it went into a slow decline, increasingly neutralised by the elite's response to some popular grievances (including the repeal of the Corn Laws in 1846), the lack of effective leadership and the movement's tendency to divide into personality-based

Further women's suffrage petitions were presented by Mill and others as the Commons debated the 1867 Reform Act, which extended the franchise to a significant proportion of working-class men in borough constituencies. On 20 May 1867, Mill moved that the word "person" be substituted for

"man" in one of this Act's clauses, but was defeated by 196 votes to 75. The MPs who voted with Mill were largely Liberals, but included a dozen Conservatives. Despite its defeat, Mill's amendment had successfully put women's suffrage on the parliamentary agenda.

This activity coincided with the beginnings of an organised women's suffrage movement. Following earlier efforts in the city by Elizabeth Wolstenholme Elmy, the Manchester National Society for Women's Suffrage held its first meeting in January 1867. Lydia Becker became its secretary and Richard Pankhurst (future husband of Emmeline) was among its earliest supporters. Also founded in 1867 were the London National Society for Women's Suffrage, whose first executive committee included Millicent Garrett Fawcett, and the Edinburgh National Society for Women's Suffrage. These regional bodies formed a loose federation, the National Society for Women's Suffrage (NSWS), in November 1867, which was joined by organisations from other towns, including Bristol and Birmingham. Local campaigners held meetings, wrote articles for the press, distributed literature and lobbied potential supporters. Between February and June 1868, 75 petitions with almost 50,000 signatures were sent to the Commons. In 1870, the *Women's Suffrage Journal* began publication with Lydia Becker as editor, continuing until her death in 1890.

In 1867, Lily Maxwell, a Manchester shopkeeper, became the first woman known to cast a parliamentary vote in modern times. Having accidentally been put on the electoral register, she voted for the victorious Liberal, Jacob Bright, at a by-election that November.

Lydia Becker subsequently co-ordinated a campaign to register other women who possessed the required property qualification, since under an 1850 act, legislation applying to men was also held to include women. Thousands of women across the country lodged claims, but most were rejected by the local courts which oversaw the registers. In November 1868, judges in the Chorlton v. Lings case ruled that the 1867 Reform Act did not include women. This did not prevent a small number of them from voting at the general election later that month, but struck a decisive blow against future claims.

After Mill lost his seat in 1868, other sympathetic MPs promoted the women's suffrage cause in the Commons. Jacob Bright, the Liberal MP for Manchester and brother of the leading Radical John Bright, was one of the most prominent, bolstered by his sister, Priscilla Bright McLaren, and his wife, Ursula Mellor Bright, both very active campaigners. In 1870, Bright introduced the first women's suffrage bill, to enfranchise female householders on the same basis as men. His speech on the second reading of the bill, which was carried by 124 votes to 91, summarised several key arguments for female enfranchisement. He considered it unjust for women to pay tax, yet be denied representation, and for propertied and intelligent women to be excluded from the franchise while men of inferior position and character possessed it. Women, he argued, had been entrusted with the local government vote without adverse effects, and were already engaged in parliamentary politics, through petitioning or following debates from the Ladies' Gallery. Bright contended

that: "to tell me that women should not be political is to tell me that they should have no care for the future of their children, no interest in the greatness and progress of their country". Despite his initial success, opponents subsequently rallied to defeat his bill.

Petitioning by women's suffrage organisations expanded during the 1870s, when petitions with over 2,200,000 signatures were presented. There was only one year in the decade when women's suffrage was not debated in the Commons, although no other bill progressed as far as in 1870. Press reports and public meetings generated publicity and support for the women's cause. But the campaign was disadvantaged by relying on private members' bills to press their claims, since backbench legislative efforts stood less chance of success than government-endorsed reforms. The introduction of a reform bill by William Gladstone's Liberal ministry in 1884 provided an opportunity to attach female suffrage to a broader, and government-

backed, measure. William Woodall, Liberal MP for Stoke-on-Trent, moved an amendment to the bill in June. But it was rejected by 271 votes to 135: the opposition of Prime Minister William Gladstone, who argued that including this divisive issue would give the Lords an excuse to block franchise reform altogether, prompted some pro-suffrage Liberal MPs to put party loyalty first and vote against Woodall's amendment. The disappointment was added to by the large increase in the male electorate under the 1884-5 Reform Act, enfranchising groups such as agricultural labourers, and reinforcing the suffragists' sense of injustice at women's political exclusion.

WOMEN IN LOCAL GOVERNMENT AND CAMPAIGNING

Despite their exclusion from parliamentary elections, women were nevertheless able to participate as voters – and, in some cases, candidates – for local government. In 1869, thanks to an amendment to the Municipal

"Shake off that apathy and timidity"

Elizabeth Neesom

Franchise Act proposed by Jacob Bright, women in England and Wales who were ratepayers were enabled to vote in municipal council elections. (Women in Scotland and Ireland had to wait until 1882 and 1898 respectively.) Following doubts about whether married women could qualify, an 1872 judgement restricted the franchise to single and widowed women. This reflected the fact that married women's property rights were subsumed in those of their husbands. From 1870 women with the relevant property qualification were allowed to vote for and be elected to School Boards, which oversaw the local administration of education. The small number of women elected to School Boards in 1870 included Lydia Becker in Manchester and Elizabeth Garrett and Emily Davies in London. Wales's first female School Board member was Rose Crawshay (Merthyr, 1871) and Scotland's was Jane Arthur (Paisley, 1873). In 1875, Martha Merrington in Kensington was the first woman elected to a Board of Guardians, which supervised administration of the poor law. By 1885 there were 50 female poor law guardians, mostly in urban areas.

Women could also vote for the new county councils created in 1888, but following legal objections to the election of two women, Jane Cobden and Margaret Sandhurst, to the first London County Council in 1889, they were not allowed to stand as candidates until 1907. Women received further opportunities under the 1894 Local Government Act. This allowed them to vote for and stand for election to rural and urban district councils and parish councils, and made it easier for them to stand as poor law guardians, by removing the high property qualification. Most significantly, it allowed married women to become local government electors, provided they did not register for the same property as their husbands. By the late 1890s there were 729,000 female voters in England and Wales, comprising 13.7 per cent of the municipal electorate. In 1895 there were 128 female School Board members and 893 female poor law guardians. While it could be argued that the responsibilities of local bodies – for education, the poor and health – were an extension of women's traditional domestic role, the local government arena was significant in giving women experience as voters and office-holders.

Although female involvement in parliamentary elections was not new, women acquired a far more significant role after the 1883 Corrupt Practices Act. This measure limited election spending by candidates and restricted the number of paid election workers. Candidates had to rely instead on voluntary help from supporters, which became increasingly necessary after the electorate was enlarged in 1884. Through extended party organisations in the constituencies, women (and men) were enlisted to perform essential electioneering tasks such as clerical work and canvassing voters. In 1883, the Primrose League was founded to support the Conservative cause, and became the largest mass political organisation of its day, encompassing men, women and children. By 1891 it had 500,000 female members and these "Primrose Dames" were praised by Conservative candidates for their electioneering efforts.

While the Primrose League did not take an official position on women's suffrage, the main Conservative organisation, the National Union of Conservative and Constitutional Associations, passed resolutions backing female enfranchisement in 1887, 1889, 1891 and 1894, and the party's leader, Lord Salisbury, spoke favourably on women's suffrage in 1888. It was generally felt that if women were enfranchised on the same basis as men – giving the vote largely to propertied middle-class women – this would be to the Conservatives' advantage. It was not only Liberal backbenchers who brought forward women's suffrage bills, but also Conservatives, such as William Forsyth in 1874 and Sir Albert Rollit in 1892. Generally speaking, though, the Conservative leadership was more sympathetic towards women's suffrage than were the party's rank-and-file MPs. The reverse was true of the Liberals.

To the Right Honourable, the Lords Spiritual and Temporal of Great Britain and Ireland in Parliament assembled.

The humble Petition of the undersigned the Head Mistress & Assistant-Mistresses of the Dulwich High School,

Sheweth

That a measure is now before Parliament for extending the Franchise to all men householders in the United Kingdom.

That by this Bill two millions of the least educated section of the Community will be added to the electorate; while educated and intelligent women, who are heads of households, are excluded from the operation of the Bill, although they contribute equally with men to the taxation of the Country.

That among the persons so excluded are women landowners, who form one seventh of the land proprietors of the country; women of means and position living on their own property, schoolmistresses and other Teachers, women farmers, merchants, manufacturers and shopkeepers, besides large numbers of self supporting women engaged in other occupations. They believe that the claim of these householders for admission within the pale of the Constitution is as reasonable as that of the County Householders, and that they would be at least equal in general and political intelligence to the great body of agricultural and other labourers who are to be enfranchised by the Government Bill.

That the injustice of excluding women householders from representation would be greatly intensified by the operation of the new service franchise, under which the servants of a Lady, living in houses for which she paid rent and taxes, would have the vote in right of the occupation of those houses while she herself, though the head of the household would have no vote.

Wherefore your Petitioners humbly pray that in any measure which may be submitted to your Right Honourable House, for amending the Law relating to the Representation of the People, your Lordships will make such provision as shall seem expedient for the exercise of the Franchise by duly qualified women.

And your Petitioners will ever pray &c.

Mary Alger	High School for Girls, Dulwich		
L. J. Gunner	High School for Girls West Dulwich	Margaret Morison	High School for Girls W. Dulwich
Clara Arnold	High School for Girls West Dulwich	Grace Bushnell	High School for Girls W. Dulwich
Helen Onions	High School for Girls W. Dulwich	Louisa Brassine	High School for Girls W. Dulwich
Dora Knight	High School for Girls	Catherine A. Jones	High School for Girls " "
Mary E. Swindells	High School for Girls	Mary A. Burrell	High School for Girls " "
Lenore Evansfield	High School for Girls " "	William Wynne	High School for Girls " "
Ada B. Hurrell	High School for Girls " "	Humphrey Hark	High School for Girls " "
Emily Collyns	High School for Girls " "		
Maud M. Eccott	High School for Girls " "		
Anna Barth	High School for Girls		
Sarah Lukes	High School for Girls "		
Gertrude Smith	High School for Girls "		
Ida Salvage	High School for Girls "		
Bertha J. Taylor	High School for Girls "		
Alice Russell	High School for Girls "		

Right
Petition from the Mistresses of Dulwich High School, 1884. This rare surviving original women's suffrage petition to Parliament was presented to the House of Lords during the passage of the Third Reform Bill

The Liberals too sought to harness female support, although women's suffrage proved a divisive issue for Liberal party organisation. Founded in 1887 as a federation of 63 local women's Liberal associations, by 1895 the Women's Liberal Federation (which favoured women's suffrage) had 448 branches with 82,000 members. However, opponents of women's suffrage had split off to found the Women's National Liberal Association in 1892. Although their electioneering assistance offered women potential leverage over candidates, in 1896, the Women's Liberal Federation declined to make women's suffrage a test question, leaving it to local branches to decide whether to campaign for candidates who failed to endorse it. Not until December 1897 – with Gladstone no longer party leader – did the General Committee of the main party organisation, the National Liberal Federation, endorse women's suffrage.

Although trade unions were often heavily influenced by the demands of male breadwinners, relegating women to domestic roles, women did participate in the trade union movement, both in women-only bodies, such as the Leeds Tailoresses Union (1889), and in mixed organisations, such as the Northern Counties Amalgamated Association of Cotton Weavers, two-thirds of whose membership was female by the 1890s. However, organisations such as the Women's Trade Union Association, founded in 1889 by Clementina Black, struggled to sustain support from low-paid female workers. The Social Democratic Federation, founded in 1884, and the Independent Labour Party, established in 1893, both admitted women as members on an equal basis with men. The Independent Labour Party's 1895 conference passed a resolution in support of extending electoral rights for both men and women. However, for the burgeoning labour movement, wider socialist objectives had a higher priority than parliamentary reform.

THE MATCHWOMEN AND THE BOW STRIKE, 1888

Against all the odds, working women still came together to fight their exploitation in the workplace. A major turning-point came with the Bryant & May strike of 1888 in Bow, in the heart of London's East End. Bow's respectable residents already felt they had a good deal to put up with from Bryant & May's matchwomen, who liked to travel arm-in-arm in noisy female gangs, "cheeking" passers-by and using distinctly unladylike language. They personified the new and alarming figure of the "factory girl", often presented in middle-class accounts as a tough, belligerent virago who struck fear into the hearts of the "respectable", whilst also possessing a dark sexual allure.

The Bow matchwomen's walkout from their factory in the summer of 1888 was sparked by a dispute over their appalling working conditions. They had no union,

Above

Striking women workers from the Bryant and May factory

no resources, and no status. When Fabian journalist Annie Besant exposed the horrors of their work, including the industrial disease phosphorus necrosis (the dreaded "phossy jaw" to the matchwomen themselves), the firm reacted furiously, demanding all workers sign a paper stating the claims were false. Despite knowing that they faced immediate dismissal, they refused to sign. Bryant & May then made a serious miscalculation, sacking one young matchwoman in an attempt to intimidate the others. Instead, her workmates simply downed tools and followed her. Outside the factory gates, they organised themselves into a committee, and began picketing the factory.

Soon a 1,400-strong strike force was parading the streets, singing unflattering songs about their employers, and collecting funds from passers-by, who threw coins which the women deftly caught in their white work-aprons. The secret of their unexpected victory lay in solidarity, sisterhood – and hats. Their unwritten code insisted first and foremost upon loyalty among workmates. If a woman was sacked or ill, her workmates would put up a collection to help her. Occasional disagreements were settled outside the factory, with quick but decisive fist fights: local police declined to interfere. The women took a defiant pride in their appearance, developing their own styles and fashions – always topped off with huge and colourful feathered hats, which they shared, paying into a "feather club" to buy them. These things helped foster a strong sense of identity, and signalled a refusal to be either unseen or unheard.

"THE RIGHTS of WOMEN" or the EFFECTS of FEMAL

Above

The Rights of Women or the Effects of Female Enfranchisement, by George Cruikshank (1852). This satirical scene of an election husting highlights concerns surrounding women's suffrage in the mid-19th century, including women being swayed by physically attractive candidates and influencing their husband's political activities

Local papers initially sided with the "gentlemen" employers, but the women turned the tide with astonishing speed. Marching to Parliament, they told their story to MPs, and an independent report proved conditions at the factory to be even worse than Besant's exposé had suggested. Share prices began to tumble, and the employers were forced to give in to the women's demands for better pay and conditions, and the right to form the largest union of women and girls in the country. The extraordinary victory by the poorest women workers marked a turning point in Britain's industrial history. Other similarly-exploited workers followed suit, using strike action to demand the right to unionise. They spread the message to other women, holding meetings for workers in nearby jam factories and confectionery works.

TENSIONS AND SPLITS

Despite the success of the matchwomen, frustration at the failure to make progress on suffrage – particularly after the 1884-5 Reform Act broadened

the franchise for men but again failed to include women – led to growing tensions within the women's suffrage movement. Several issues caused divisions among campaigners during this period, some more serious than others. The National Society for Women's Suffrage (NSWS) split in the early 1870s over the relationship between the suffrage campaign and Josephine Butler's Ladies' National Association for the Repeal of the Contagious Diseases Acts. Some feared that the involvement of prominent suffragists with the campaign against the Acts might undermine the respectability of the suffrage cause. This, and tensions with the Manchester suffragists, prompted the London National Society for Women's Suffrage to decline to join a new Central Committee of the NSWS in 1872, although it did eventually do so in 1877. In 1888, there were divisions over proposed changes to the NSWS's rules to allow women's Liberal associations to affiliate. While most members endorsed this, some, including Millicent Fawcett and Lydia Becker, objected to

While the early suffrage campaign largely involved middle-class women, the 1890s saw efforts to attract wider support. Spurred by the progress of a women's suffrage bill in 1892 – when the majority against its second reading was just 23 votes – the various women's suffrage bodies united to organise a "Special Appeal". Particular efforts were made to circulate it to working-class women, including through the Women's Co-operative Guild. Esther Roper, secretary of the Manchester Society for Women's Suffrage, collected signatures from local textile workers by holding meetings at factory gates during dinner breaks. It became the largest Parliamentary petition since the 1840s, with over 250,000 signatures, and was displayed in Westminster Hall in May 1896 to show MPs the weight of support for women's suffrage.

In February 1897, a women's suffrage bill introduced by the Conservative Ferdinand Faithfull Begg received loud cheers in the Commons when it passed its second reading by 228 votes to 157. The number of MPs voting for women's suffrage was more than three times what it had been in 1867, demonstrating the progress made in building up support. But Begg's bill progressed no further: greater efforts were required if a women's suffrage bill was to pass through Parliament. However, a new phase in the campaign for votes for women was about to begin with the establishment of the National Union of Women's Suffrage Societies.

In another way, though, women were already becoming more visible in the Palace of Westminster, increasingly working as secretaries to MPs. In 1895 the House of Commons decided to establish an in-house typing service, and the firm of Ashworth & Co won the contract to provide it. It was run by May Ashworth, who had set up her own business down the road in Victoria Street in 1888. The Serjeant-at-Arms gave permission for Ashworth to keep in the typewriting room at the House of Commons as many machines as she thought necessary, and to place a sufficient staff of skilled operators also qualified to write shorthand at the disposal of MPs. She would go on to expand and run the service through marriage, divorce and wartime to her death in 1928, and Ashworth & Co continued to work in Parliament until after the Second World War. In 1897 Ashworth described how "an MP rushes into our room and begins at once to dictate something or another", and MPs often expressed "wonderment at the great speed obtained by the girls". Yet despite Westminster becoming increasingly dependent on women, it would take two further decades of campaigning before they obtained the vote.

abandoning the society's non-party stance, prompting a split into two rival bodies.

Another thorny question was whether to seek the vote for married women (who under the principle of "coverture" had no separate legal identity from their husbands) or for single and widowed women only. The women's suffrage bills brought forward from the 1870s took varying approaches. One compromise solution was to enfranchise women on the same basis as men, which would exclude married women while the franchise was property-based, but kept open the possibility of future enfranchisement. Some suffragists, however, wanted a clear commitment to enfranchising married women, as well as spinsters and widows, notably Elizabeth Wolstenholme Elmy, who founded the Women's Franchise League in 1889. Alongside internal divisions, suffragists faced the emergence of female anti-suffrage efforts, such as the 1889 "Appeal against the Extension of the Parliamentary Franchise to Women", signed by 104 prominent women led by Mary, Mrs Humphry Ward.

ESCAPING THE CAGE, 1897–1918

Although by the beginning of the 20th century some progress had been made, success was still frustratingly far away. Other issues, notably the Irish question, convulsed the political world, and the increasing control of the political parties, with their own agendas, over Parliament limited the opportunities for individual MPs to push for change. Yet by the time the 19th century drew to a close, the suffragists (which at this stage meant all those who supported the "Votes for Women" campaign) shared a common hope that victory was in sight. Women were now more prominent in public life and party politics than they had been 30 years before, and the now fairly broad enjoyment of the franchise by working men made it even more difficult to argue that women's continued exclusion was justifiable.

Krista Cowman
Jane Robinson
Mari Takayanagi

THE SUFFRAGISTS: THE NUWSS

There were already differences of objective and tactics which would bedevil the movement for women's suffrage. Different groups had different interpretations of what victory might mean: a vote for unmarried women on the same terms as it was already granted to men; a vote including married women, or a universal vote for men and women over 21 (or 30, or 35). What mattered to everyone, however, was breaking that most intransigent of barriers: any Parliamentary vote for any woman at all.

In October 1896, representatives of women's suffrage committees and societies across the British Isles came together in Birmingham to discuss their strategy before the final push. Regional groups had done all they could since 1866 to further the campaign for the vote, but were stymied by a lack of funds and coordination. A year later, the National Union of Women's Suffrage Societies (NUWSS) was born; a nationwide, non-militant, non-party body of activists both male and female (but mostly the latter) which at its height numbered 600 branches and over 100,000 members. They are the people we now remember as suffragists, as opposed to their more militant sisters, the suffragettes. Officers of the NUWSS at national and regional level were seasoned in public service through work as Poor-Law Guardians, School Board members and town council electors. At their head was Millicent Fawcett (1847–1929).

Fawcett was the younger sister of Elizabeth Garrett Anderson, the first woman to qualify and practice as a doctor in Britain. She was brought up in a Liberal Suffolk household and educated at an "Academy for the Daughters of Gentlemen" in London, leaving at the age of 15. Introduced to the Victorian women's movement by her elder sisters, in 1867 she married Cambridge professor and eminent Liberal MP Henry Fawcett, 14 years her senior, and blind. Millicent Fawcett flourished as a political and academic amanuensis to her husband, a campaigner for higher education for women and increasingly an activist for women's political rights. Full of common sense and enthusiasm, she was also an indomitable optimist – an essential quality for coping with the repeated disappointments of the suffrage campaign. Those were gifts; she worked hard to acquire complementary accomplishments to help her develop into an excellent administrator and public speaker, firstly to aid her husband, and secondly to arm herself in the fight for the vote.

Mrs Fawcett developed a strategy of lobbying sympathetic Parliamentary members and candidates, garnering all-party support for constitutional change and educating public opinion about the campaign and its significance to individuals and their communities. This the NUWSS did through disseminating literature via regional branches, publishing a national journal *The Common Cause*, and encouraging members to hold meetings in towns and on tours of rural areas. Within a few years, however, a division began to emerge about how best to undertake the fight, with the foundation of Emmeline Pankhurst's Women's Social and Political Union (WSPU) in 1903. The WSPU would become frustrated with what was seen as the complacency and lack of proactivity within the ranks of the NUWSS, though it was only when a journalist from the *Daily Mail* coined the term "suffragette" in 1906 that a distinction began to emerge between militant and non-militant activists, or the suffragettes of the WSPU and the suffragists of the NUWSS. Very broadly speaking, the WSPU became more involved in protest while the NUWSS concentrated on demonstration.

Mrs Fawcett was at first supportive of Emmeline Pankhurst and her suffragettes, hosting a banquet at the Savoy for ten recently-released WSPU members imprisoned for attempting to storm the Palace of Westminster in 1906. "Far from having injured the movement," Mrs Fawcett insisted, "they have done more during the last twelve months to bring it within the realms of practical politics than we have been able to accomplish in the same number of years." But as the militancy of the WSPU increased in intensity over the next years, suffragists began to distance themselves from direct action, feeling uncomfortable with (though not always unsympathetic to) the suffragettes' tactics

Right
Emmeline Pankhurst
(1858–1928), by John
H F Bacon, c.1908

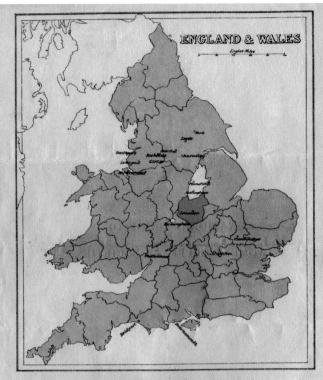

ENGLAND & WALES

AREAS of the various Societies.

☐ = North of England Society for Women's Suffrage. Secretary : Miss Roper, 5, John Dalton Street, Manchester.

☐ = Central and East of England Society for Women's Suffrage. Secretary: Miss Palliser, 10, Great College Street, London, S.W.

☐ = Central and Western Society for Women's Suffrage. Secretary : Mrs. Charles Baxter, 39, Victoria Street, London, S.W.

☐ = Bristol and West of England Society for Women's Suffrage. Office : 69, Park Street, Bristol.

☐ = Leicester Society.

☐ Nottinghamshire Nottingham and Mansfield Societies.

○ Birmingham and the district for 20 miles round Birmingham Society.

The Societies in Leeds, York, Halifax, Liverpool, Birkenhead and Wirral, Southport, Rochdale, Gorton, Cambridge, Luton, Bridport, Cheltenham, Bournemouth, and Barnsley, undertake the work in their own districts, but are in connection with the main Society in whose area they are situated.

The London constituencies are divided between the Central and East of England Society and the Central and Western Society for Women's Suffrage.

National Union of Women's Suffrage Societies.

WITH a view to the more systematic and combined organisation of the work throughout the country, a National Union of Women's Suffrage Societies has been formed on the lines of the scheme adopted at the Birmingham Conference of 1896, by which England was divided for organising purposes into four large territorial areas, one of which was allotted to each of the four chief Societies.

Since the close of 1895 there has been in existence a representative Committee, consisting of delegates at first from the two Women's Suffrage Societies whose offices are in London, and from the Manchester Society, and at a later date from Edinburgh, Bristol, and other Societies. This Committee was found to be of considerable practical utility in facilitating combined action for Parliamentary work, and in other ways, and it has now taken a more definite and permanent form in the National Union.

The geographical division of work, which forms the basis of the present Union, has led to the modification of the names of several of its constituent Societies, whose titles will in future indicate their special sphere of work. Thus the Central Committee of the National Society for Women's Suffrage becomes "The Central and East of England Society," the Central National Society becomes the "Central and Western," and the Manchester National becomes the "North of England Society."

It is hoped that this Union will shortly become completely representative of every active non-party Suffrage Society in the United Kingdom.

It will easily be seen that organisation on so extensive a scale must involve extended work in each area, and therefore increased expenditure, and the Committee of the Central and Western Society earnestly hope that the friends of the movement will give them that liberal support which alone can enable them to carry out such an enterprise successfully in the large district which they have undertaken.

M. M. RUSSELL COOKE, *Treasurer.*
MARIE LOUISE BAXTER, *Secretary.*

CENTRAL AND WESTERN SOCIETY
FOR WOMEN'S SUFFRAGE,
39, VICTORIA STREET, WESTMINSTER, S.W.

Nov., 1897.

Above
Notice of the formation of the National Union of Women's Suffrage Societies, November 1897. The map shows the national coverage of the NUWSS from its earliest days

Right
NUWSS lapel pin. The union was keen to make clear its independence from political parties and constitutional approach

"We are here, not because we are law-breakers; we are here in our efforts to become law-makers"

Emmeline Pankhurst

and with the vitriol they attracted in the press. Suffragists tried to counter the popular image of mentally chaotic womanhood by campaigning in a demonstrably responsible fashion. However passionate they felt about the cause, they were aware that such passion was all too easily dismissed as hysteria. Suffragists were highly skilled at salvaging advantage whenever they could until they had accumulated success. They did not storm any citadels, nor did Mrs Fawcett lead her followers into battle. Instead she tried to persuade the opposition to work cooperatively. For her, women's suffrage was not a matter for fiery revolution but an evolutionary certainty.

THE SUFFRAGETTES: THE WSPU

The WSPU had its origins in Manchester and in Labour politics. It was set up in October 1903 at the initiative of Mrs Emmeline Pankhurst and some women members of the Manchester Independent Labour Party (ILP). Pankhurst (1858–1928), like Fawcett, had had various connections to the Victorian feminist movement, and had married a socialist and campaigner for women's suffrage who was considerably older than her. Emmeline's leading role in suffrage politics came after the death of her husband in 1898. Her small union spent much of its first two years campaigning for the vote in and around Manchester. Although it attracted little national publicity at first, its methods were quite different from those of the older, more sedate suffrage societies, and borrowed heavily from the street politics of the ILP. WSPU women speakers stood on chairs to address impromptu gatherings, boldly challenging hecklers in a way that many contemporary observers found shocking. The organisation came to national attention in October 1905. Emmeline's daughter Christabel and Annie Kenney, a young working-class woman, attended a Liberal party meeting at

Manchester's Free Trade Hall. During question time they persistently demanded an answer from the senior politician Sir Edward Grey on whether a Liberal government would give votes to women. They were thrown out of the hall and arrested on the pavement outside when they attempted to address the growing crowd. At Manchester Police Court they refused to pay a fine, and were sent to Strangeways Prison for a week.

The event made national headlines. The WSPU had become news and was determined to capitalise on its new status. Suffragettes pursued leading cabinet ministers throughout the North West, disrupting election meetings with questions, leaflets and handbells. Recognising that maintaining a high-profile campaign would require continued proximity to key political figures, the union moved its headquarters to London. Parliament – where the election had produced a huge Liberal majority – became a key focus for its activities. In February 1906 Annie Kenney organised the WSPU's first large London demonstration, coinciding with the King's speech at the opening of Parliament. Over 3,000 women, many of them carrying babies, attended a meeting at Caxton Hall in Westminster where Emmeline Pankhurst urged them to abandon the old constitutional methods of campaigning and follow her to the House of Commons. The women walked in small groups to comply with an Act of 1817 that prevented open-air meetings within the immediate vicinity of Parliament. The event passed peacefully, but the following October saw a shift in the WSPU's attitude to Parliamentary protests. A large number of women, many from outside London, gathered in St Stephen's Hall and Central Lobby in the Houses of Parliament on the day of the King's speech. Mary Gawthorpe, the WSPU's Lancashire organiser, climbed behind the statue of Stafford Northcote, the Earl of Iddesleigh, to lead the cries of "votes for women", which were audible in the chamber

of the House of Commons itself. Twelve women were arrested. In December 1906 the union attempted to repeat their protest, but this time the police response was more immediate and they were only able to get as far as Old Palace Yard before they were removed. There were five further arrests.

THE LIBERAL GOVERNMENT AND THE SUFFRAGETTES, 1906–11

The pressure that women placed on Parliament from 1906 onwards was partly the result of disappointed expectations. Many women had believed that the resignation of the Conservatives in 1905 and the subsequent election, by a landslide majority, of a Liberal government, would be likely to lead relatively quickly to enfranchisement. The Liberal party had been historically (though far from universally) more sympathetic to the cause than had the Conservatives who had been in power since 1895; and in 1906 they arrived in

government following a pact with Labour, which included some of the women's strongest allies, including the party's leader, James Keir Hardie, and George Lansbury. But while a majority in both parties were sympathetic in principle to women's suffrage, and there were plenty of Conservative MPs who supported it, the obstacles continued to be formidable. Some Conservatives would accept the enfranchisement of better-off and propertied women; but a majority of the Labour party balked at accepting partial enfranchisement of women on the basis of property qualification, insisting on the franchise for all adults, regardless of their property. The Liberals were committed to further electoral reform, but they too were divided about its nature. The issue was complicated by continuing arguments surrounding Irish Home Rule (devolution) – a subject which had split the party in the 1890s – and quickly obscured by the government's increasing difficulties with the House of Lords. Compared to their other difficulties, to the principal Liberal politicians, votes for women seemed a minor issue; and while many senior figures in the party, including the prime minister, Sir Henry Campbell-Bannerman, were supportive, others were actively hostile.

One of the hostile Liberals was Herbert Asquith, who in 1908 replaced Campbell-Bannerman as prime minister. He made it clear that he had no intention of legislating for women's suffrage, nor of helping on its way a private members' bill, despite the support of other Liberals. All he would concede was that when the government was ready to legislate on further electoral reform, if ordinary members wanted to bring in an amendment to the bill that would allow women to vote, it would not oppose it. However it was clear that no such bill was likely to be brought forward soon, and the government soon became embroiled in other disputes, notably the bitter confrontation with the House of Lords over the 1909 budget of Chancellor of the Exchequer David Lloyd George, and the subsequent two elections of 1910.

Throughout, the WSPU sought to maintain its pressure on the government and bring its cause to the attention of the public. Its demonstration in December 1906 would set a pattern for a decade of suffragette engagement with Parliament. From February 1907 the WSPU organised a series of "Women's Parliaments"; highly symbolic affairs, designed to emphasise the entirely male membership of the Westminster Parliament.

Right
Keir Hardie (1856–1915),
by Cosmo Rowe, c.1907.
A friend of the Pankhurst
family and an active
supporter of their cause,
he spoke regularly in the
Commons on suffrage issues

With every good wish for 1907 and all the coming years

J. Keir Hardie

Below
Emmeline and Christabel Pankhurst
together with Mrs Drummond were
prosecuted for the "rush" and subsequently
imprisoned. This medal awarded to Mrs
Pankhurst on her release from Holloway
prison identifies the location of her cell,
H (Hospital block), Floor 2, cell 4

MISS C. PANKHURST AT TRAFALGAR SQUARE INVITING THE AUDIENCE TO "RUSH"
THE HOUSE OF COMMONS ON OCTOBER 13.
The National Women's Social and Political Union,
4, Clements Inn, W.C.

MRS. PANKHURST AT TRAFALGAR SQUARE INVITING THE AUDIENCE TO "RUSH"
THE HOUSE OF COMMONS ON OCTOBER 13.
The National Women's Social and Political Union.

MRS. DRUMMOND AT TRAFALGAR SQUARE INVITING THE AUDIENCE TO "RUSH"
THE HOUSE OF COMMONS ON OCTOBER 13.
The National Women's Social and Political Union,
4, Clements Inn, W.C.

ARREST OF MRS. PANKHURST, MISS PANKHURST, AND MRS. DRUMMOND,
MR. JARVIS READING THE WARRANT AT CLEMENT'S INN, OCTOBER 13, 1908.
The National Women's Social and Political Union, 4, Clements Inn, W.C.

Above

The WSPU arranged for postcards to be issued publicising the "rush" campaign. One shows the Pankhursts and Mrs Drummond being arrested. Postcards published by Sandle Brothers, London

WSPU branches from all over the country sent delegates. Branch collections covered delegates' train fares, something that led to accusations in the press that they were paid agitators. Women's Parliaments would meet in Caxton Hall, close to the Palace of Westminster, at a time designed to coincide with a specific event such as the state opening of Parliament, the King's speech or a women's suffrage debate. They ended by endorsing a resolution that would then be taken to Parliament by small groups of delegates. Large numbers of police would be deployed to keep women out of the building. There were always high numbers of arrests. Occasionally deputations breached police lines. In one ruse, at the third Women's Parliament in February 1908 the WSPU hired two furniture removal vans, which disgorged twenty-one women at the entrance.

Women's Parliaments attracted much publicity. The sight of large numbers of women, well-dressed wealthy ladies and Northern factory workers in shawls and clogs, brawling with the police in Palace Yard, fascinated the photo journalists who worked for popular titles such as the *Daily Mirror*. The arrests drew attention to the spread of support for the WSPU's demands; after the Women's Parliament of February 1908, the *Daily Mail* noted the presence of women from Bradford, Bury,

Leeds, Halifax, Preston, Stoke-on-Trent, Liverpool, Hanley, Glasgow, Chester, Manchester and Rochdale. Women's Parliaments were not exclusively WSPU events. Members of the Women's Freedom League (WFL), the militant suffrage organisation led by Charlotte Despard, Teresa Billington-Greig and Edith How-Martyn that split off from the WSPU in November 1907, joined in and also organised their own Parliamentary protests. A number of other suffrage societies that supported direct militant actions, including the Actresses' Franchise League and the Church League for Women's Suffrage, were represented at the ten Women's Parliaments held between February 1907 and November 1911. In 1908 the WSPU adopted the colours purple, green and white. Used in processions and merchandise, the branding proved enormously successful. Other suffrage societies devised their own colour schemes: the NUWSS was red, green and white; the WFL was green, white and gold.

One of the largest demonstrations came in October 1908. To attract wider support for the fifth Women's Parliament in October 1908, the WSPU printed a handbill that invited the public to "Help the Suffragettes to Rush the House of Commons". Emmeline and Christabel Pankhurst and Flora Drummond were arrested and gaoled for producing the leaflet, and were

"Help the Suffragettes to Rush the House of Commons"

Right
Plaque marking Emily
Wilding Davison's overnight
stay in Parliament on
census night 1911, placed
in the Chapel of St Mary
Undercroft cupboard by
Tony Benn MP in 1988

IN LOVING MEMORY OF
EMILY WILDING DAVISON

IN THIS BROOM CUPBOARD EMILY WILDING DAVISON HID HERSELF, ILLEGALLY, DURING THE NIGHT OF THE 1911 CENSUS.
SHE WAS A BRAVE SUFFRAGETTE CAMPAIGNING FOR VOTES FOR WOMEN AT A TIME WHEN PARLIAMENT DENIED THEM THAT RIGHT.
IN THIS WAY SHE WAS ABLE TO RECORD HER ADDRESS, ON THE NIGHT OF THAT CENSUS, AS BEING "THE HOUSE OF COMMONS", THUS MAKING HER CLAIM TO THE SAME POLITICAL RIGHTS AS MEN.
EMILY WILDING DAVISON DIED IN JUNE 1913 FROM INJURIES SUSTAINED WHEN SHE THREW HERSELF UNDER THE KING'S HORSE AT THE DERBY TO DRAW PUBLIC ATTENTION TO THE INJUSTICE SUFFERED BY WOMEN.
BY SUCH MEANS WAS DEMOCRACY WON FOR THE PEOPLE OF BRITAIN.

Notice placed here by Tony Benn MP

"I must tell you, Mr. Speaker, that I am going to put a plaque in the House, I shall have it made myself and screwed on the door of the broom cupboard in the Crypt."

thus unable to participate in determined but unsuccessful attempts to penetrate the police cordon outside Parliament on the day chosen, 13 October 1908. Nevertheless, Margaret Travers Symons, a member of the WSPU, managed to get onto the floor of the House while MPs were debating the Children's Bill. As Keir Hardie's secretary she was able to watch proceedings through a "peephole" in the door to the Chamber, and ran inside. Her words, "Leave off discussing the children and attend to women first! Votes for women!" were widely reported at home and abroad, and officially recorded in Hansard. Two weeks later, on 28 October, the Women's Freedom League again attempted a large-scale protest inside and outside Parliament. Dorothy Molony climbed the base of the statue of Richard I in Old Palace Yard and addressed a large crowd of women, while male supporters protested in the Strangers' Gallery, women protested in St Stephen's Hall, and inside the Ladies' Gallery, two other Women's Freedom League members, Helen Fox and Muriel Matters, padlocked themselves to the grille that kept women out of sight of MPs in the chamber. While attendants struggled to remove them (eventually having to remove the actual grille) Violet Tillard was able to drop a banner into the debating chamber and deliver a lengthy speech that drew attention to their inferior status behind the "insulting grille" and their continued exclusion from Parliament and its processes. Others continued the protest in the yard.

Following the grille incident, the Parliamentary authorities purchased a pair of bolt-clippers. In April 1909 four WSPU suffragettes chained themselves to statues in St Stephen's Hall. Margery Hume chained herself to the statue of Viscount Falkland; the police report recorded that the clippers proved most satisfactory, although the damage caused to the Falkland's spurs can still be seen today. Another smaller-scale but successful breach of Parliamentary security was carried out by Emily Wilding Davison on census night in April 1911. Suffragettes had urged women to boycott the census, arguing that as they did not "count" enough to have a vote, then "neither shall they be counted". Some women spoiled their census forms with suffrage slogans while others spent the night in large groups and refused to fill in returns. Emily Davison chose to pass the night hiding in a broom cupboard in the House of Commons, and was duly recorded by the Clerk of Works as having been "found hiding in the crypt of Westminster Hall". Davison is known to have hidden or demonstrated in the Palace of Westminster on at least five other occasions, and had even been banned by the Speaker. Two years later,

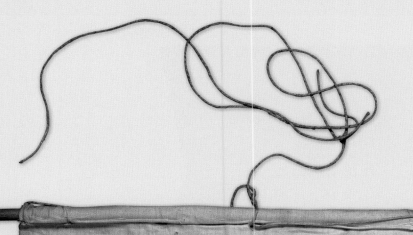

PROCLAMATION.

Whereas the Nation depends for its progress and existence upon the work and services of women as well as of men;

Whereas the State is organised for the mutual protection and co-operation of all its citizens, women as well as men;

Whereas the Government conducts the national business by means of taxes levied upon women as well as men;

Whereas the women of the Nation have made clear their need for political rights, and their desire to possess the Parliamentary Vote;

ereas working women, and women in the home, are in especial need of the protection of the Vote since legislation is interfering more and more with their interests;

the

EN'S FREEDOM LEAGUE

calls upon the Government to remove the sex-disability which deprives qualified women of their just right of voting in the Parliamentary elections, and

DEMANDS

the immediate extension of the Franchise to Women on the same terms as it is, or may be enjoyed by men.

The Nation can never be free until the law recognises and establishes

VOTES FOR WOMEN

THE DEMAND IS JUST. THE REFORM INEVITABLE.

DELAY IS UNWISE AND UNJUST.

Therefore in the Name of Liberty and Humanity the Women's Freedom League claims the Vote

THIS SESSION.

W. CONQUEST & Co., PRINTERS, TOTTENHAM.

Below, left
Proclamation banner and police report:
This Women's Freedom League banner
was unfurled in the House of Commons
on 28 October 1908 during the grille protest.
The police report of the incident names
Miss Helen Fox and Miss Muriel Matters
as responsible

6

28th October 1908

I have to report for information of the Sergt at Arms that at 8.30pm a Demonstration took place in the Ladies Gallery and St Stephens Hall also the Members Gallery simultaneously by members of the Womens Freedom League.
The following had been taken to the Ladies Gallery at about 5.30 pm by Mr. Stephen Collins M.P
Miss Helen Fox } Robert St
" Muriel Matters } Adelphi WC
Both chained themselves to the ironwork of the grill and were brought out with the ironwork and the locks were filed off in a Committee Room
The following were ejected from St Stephens Hall
Miss Henderson
" E. Bremner

Davison died following her protest at the Derby, becoming the suffragette martyr.

CONCILIATION: 1910–13

By the time of the 1910 and 1911 protests, the most significant attempt to break the deadlock had been underway for some time. Supporters of women's suffrage in the Commons set up an all-party "conciliation committee" in February 1910, headed by Lord Lytton and the journalist HN Brailsford, in an attempt to bring pro-suffrage MPs from all parties together to draft a women's suffrage bill that could be accepted by both Conservatives and Liberals. The resulting "Conciliation Bill" fell short of the WSPU's demand for votes for women on the same terms as they were given to men, but proposed using the municipal franchise qualification to enfranchise around one million women. Their bill passed a second reading and the government even agreed to allow it time to be further debated: but then the death of Edward VII and the clash with the Lords prevented further progress and resulted in the dissolution of Parliament and the second election of the year.

Suffragettes responded with a large demonstration to Parliament on the day of the dissolution, 18 November 1910 – "Black Friday". Large numbers of police were drafted into the area, and the demonstration was met with higher levels of violence than usual. Among the demonstrators was Rosa May Billinghurst, an active suffragette and wheelchair user, who was thrown from her adapted tricycle by the police. Several women were seriously injured. Winston Churchill, as Home Secretary, rejected calls for a public inquiry and was reluctant to answer questions on the matter in the House of Commons, fuelling speculation that the police brutality had been endorsed by the government.

Following the election of December 1910, which resulted in a Liberal government dependent on Labour and especially Irish nationalist support, a second

Conciliation Bill was brought in with revised terms more satisfactory to all suffrage campaigners. Given a second reading by a large margin, the government promised to provide time for it to be debated in the following session in 1912. The terms of the bill, though, were still controversial, particularly within the Liberal party, where it was seen as favourable to the Conservatives. Then in November 1911, Asquith unexpectedly announced the government's intention to introduce a Manhood Suffrage Bill that would not include women – though it could be amended to give them the vote.

Campaigners reacted with outrage. A large demonstration was called at Parliament, but, fearing a repeat of the violence of Black Friday, suffragettes simultaneously initiated a mass window-smashing campaign against government offices and commercial properties in London's West End: it was better, they said, to break windows than to break women's bodies as had happened on Black Friday. The protest was repeated in March 1912 when the Conciliation Bill was defeated – with many Liberal MPs now preferring to wait for the promised Suffrage Bill. The protests resulted in the arrests on conspiracy charges of Mrs Pankhurst and her close collaborators, Emmeline and Frederick Pethick Lawrence. Mrs Pankhurst's daughter, Christabel, evaded arrest and escaped to Paris.

The government introduced its Franchise and Registration Bill in June, placing as many obstacles in the way of the supporters of women's suffrage as they could. Their task was already difficult enough as a result of the simultaneous battle over Irish Home Rule. Tension increased further as the opportunity to amend the bill approached. In January 1913 Sir Edward Grey and David Lloyd George agreed to meet a small deputation of working women organised by Flora Drummond on behalf of the WSPU to discuss suffrage amendments to the current Reform Bill. The deputation was well-received, leaving the women feeling confident. But very shortly afterwards the Speaker's sensational ruling that it was not consistent with the House's procedures to add women's suffrage to an existing bill, and that if the amendments were passed the bill would have to be withdrawn and begin again, caused fury. When Flora Drummond's request for another meeting with Lloyd George was refused, suffragettes responded with a large demonstration to Parliament that resulted in several arrests; there were also more violent protests, among them the attempt to destroy the house being built for Lloyd George in Surrey.

CAT AND MOUSE AND THE GREAT PILGRIMAGE

The defeat of the Conciliation Bill and the mass window-smashing of 1911 and 1912 had already marked a shift in WSPU tactics. Whereas previously the union had celebrated large numbers of arrests during deputations to Parliament, it now shifted to acts of clandestine militancy, including arson. Disruption to normal patterns of life was the main aim. Women carrying out these actions were supposed to evade arrest. Women who were arrested for obstruction received only a few weeks or a month in prison, often as a result of refusing to pay a fine. But those who were arrested for arson or similarly serious forms of criminal damage faced higher sentences, often with hard labour. Many women who were imprisoned responded with hunger strikes. Prison authorities used forcible feeding, but by 1913 this was becoming problematic. A number of high-profile cases, including those of Lord Lytton's sister Lady Constance, forcibly fed when disguised as a working-class suffragette despite her weak heart, and Lilian Lenton, a young WSPU member who developed pleurisy when food was poured into her lung rather than her stomach, suggested that forcible feeding was not medically safe nor carefully monitored.

Fearing the impact of a suffragette death in prison, the Home Secretary Reginald McKenna approved a different course of action. The Prisoners' Temporary Discharge for Ill-Health Act, passed in April 1913, allowed prison authorities to release hunger-striking suffragettes when their health became a concern. Women would be released on licence, and re-arrested

as soon as they were well enough to go back to gaol. The Act was known as the "Cat and Mouse Act" as it replicated the way a hunting cat would play with a mouse prior to the final kill. The Government anticipated (correctly as it turned out) that hunger-strikers would be less than keen to return to prison once they were deemed fit. Suffragettes on licence were clandestinely photographed, tailed and monitored by police. Despite this a number managed to evade re-arrest through a network of safe houses run by suffrage supporters.

From 1912 onwards, the NUWSS and its affiliated suffragist societies abandoned their non-party stance and allied themselves to Labour candidates, believing the Liberal and Tory administrations to have squandered their chances to enfranchise women. Though a Liberal herself, Mrs Fawcett developed the Election Fighting Fund (EFF) specifically to support Labour candidates at general and by-elections. She sent countless deputations to politicians; wrote them letters; pleaded with them to admit that women were "people" in legal terms and must therefore be eligible to vote under any "Representation of the People" Bill.

In contrast to the WSPU, the NUWSS responded to the increasing frustration with a new series of peaceful demonstrations. Its committee member Mrs Katherine Harley proposed a grand gesture to break the deadlock and to rehabilitate the image of the campaign: a peaceful crusade, a march to end all marches, involving thousands of suffragists across the British Isles, culminating in a massed rally in Hyde Park. Such a spectacular event, she argued, could not fail to capture the public's imagination and convince the government that votes for women were not only desirable but inevitable. Called "the Great Pilgrimage", after just two months of frenzied organisation, the first Suffragist pilgrims set off in the summer of 1913.

Aristocrats marched shoulder-to-shoulder with colliery girls, academics with housewives, the young with the old and men with the vast majority of women: the Great Pilgrimage was about solidarity and mutual support. Wearing the suffragist colours of red, white and green, they traced major routes across the

Above

Alice Hawkins was a machinist at the Equity shoe factory in Leicester. A socialist and trade unionist, she believed women's suffrage was essential for working women's rights to be taken seriously. The mother of six children, it was possible for Alice to be an active WSPU campaigner because her husband was also a supporter. She was imprisoned five times for her role in WSPU protests. The Alice Hawkins collection, still held by her family, documents her involvement. It includes her WSPU hunger strike medal, her scrapbook, which includes a bail warrant following her arrest outside Parliament, and her extensive suffrage postcard collection

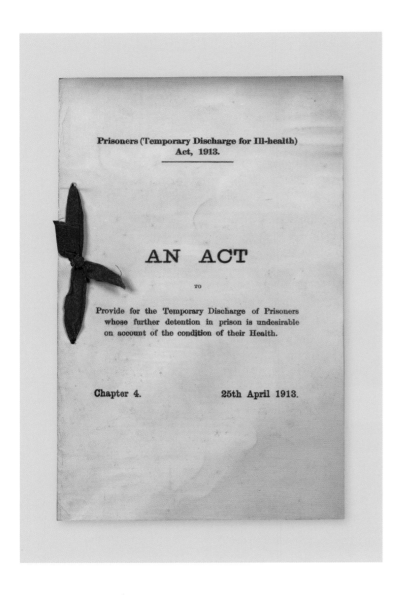

Prisoners (Temporary Discharge for Ill-health) Act, 1913.

AN ACT

TO

Provide for the Temporary Discharge of Prisoners whose further detention in prison is undesirable on account of the condition of their Health.

Chapter 4.   25th April 1913.

Above

Prisoners (Temporary Discharge for Ill-Health) Act, 1913. Aimed at hunger-striking suffragettes, it was nicknamed the "Cat and Mouse" Act

them to be arsonists and stone-throwers. To counter this, pilgrims' banners were gracefully conciliatory while still attempting to rouse support, with elaborately-embroidered slogans like "By Faith Not Force", and "Better is Wisdom than Weapons of War". When a recently-discovered banner from Keswick was unrolled for the first time, pellets of lead-shot fell from its folds, no doubt fired at the pilgrims by a furious onlooker.

The purpose of the Great Pilgrimage was to demonstrate to Parliament and the people how many "quiet, home-loving women" of Great Britain wanted the vote: that not every campaigner for women's suffrage was a rebel or a suffragette. When Mrs Fawcett and others met Prime Minister Asquith after its completion, even he had to admit that the Great Pilgrimage had proven that women did deserve to be counted as "people" after all.

A "SEX WAR"?

Journalists often wrote about the suffrage campaign in terms of a "sex war"; women's excuse for a wholesale rebellion designed to turn the world of men upside down. Certain reactionary medical men and educationalists continued to argue that if women thought too much, their wombs would wither, imperilling the physical future of the nation. Cudgelling their brains in an attempt to cast a meaningful Parliamentary vote, given their monthly "disturbances", would not only be useless but dangerous. But even some women advanced similar arguments. The National League for Opposing Woman Suffrage (NLOWS) was founded in 1910, amalgamating major men's and women's anti-suffrage societies. Among its officers were the popular novelist Mrs Humphry Ward (former president of the women's Anti-Suffrage League) and the explorer Gertrude Bell. Both were independent, high-achieving women who devoutly believed that Parliament was no place for them. Women had enough power already, they claimed, through their influence on husbands and children. Besides, the process of voting was vulgar and unfeminine. Its views were represented by another NLOWS officer, Lord Curzon, who published "Fifteen Good Reasons Against the Grant of Female Suffrage" as a manifesto. Among the reasons was the assertion that: "Women have not, as a sex, or a class, the calmness of temperament or the balance of mind, nor have they the training necessary to qualify them to exercise a weighty judgement in political affairs."

Conversely, while the Suffragettes attempted to restrict most of their Parliamentary protests to women to emphasise the distinction between their exclusion and

country: from Newcastle and Carlisle in the north, Cromer and Yarmouth in the east, Aberystwyth in Wales and Land's End, Portsmouth, Brighton and Margate in the south. Further routes fed into these main ones like tributaries, all flowing to the capital city. Many stayed the whole course, travelling as far as 300 miles during the six weeks from the middle of June to the end of July. Most pilgrims walked. Others rode in horse-drawn caravans, on horseback, in the occasional motor-car or charabanc and on bicycles.

The pilgrims had to contend with an assumption that they were associated with the militants, rendering them liable to be kicked and trampled by crowds who assumed

Above
National League for
Opposing Women's
Suffrage badge, c. 1914–15

Right
Wooden Suffragette Doll,
c. 1912–14. This very rare
doll depicts a suffragette
as a shouting harridan

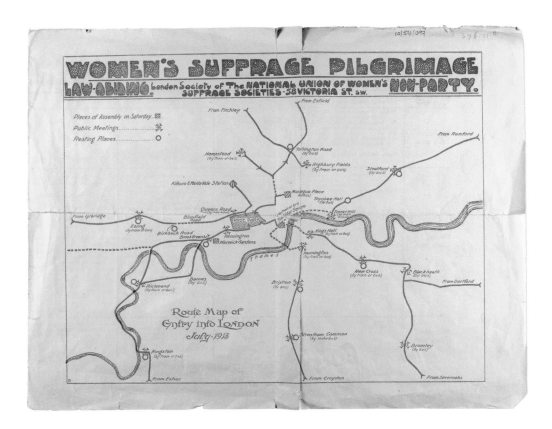

men's inclusion in parliamentary processes, sympathetic men were involved. When Marion Wallace-Dunlop carried out her individual protest by stamping the phrase "it is the right of the subject to petition the King" on the wall of St Stephen's Hall in 1909, Victor Duval, a member of the Men's Political Union (male supporters of the WSPU), helped her in the attack and was charged alongside her. Members of the Men's Political Union and the Men's League for Women's Suffrage were key witnesses to the most violent response to the protests on Black Friday in November 1910.

One of the most enduring emblems of the NUWSS was a stylised tree in the suffragist colours, with a strong trunk representing the central administration and a host of flourishing branches representing not only the regional women's suffrage societies, but a myriad of affiliated organisations. They ranged from writers', artists' or actresses' suffrage societies to those of gym-teachers and short-hand typists. There were larger groups, which defied categorisation as militant or non-militant, among them the Women's Freedom League. Activists for women's suffrage usually belonged to more than one group. Some even shared their allegiance across the divide between suffragists and suffragettes. Millicent Fawcett's sister, Dr Elizabeth Garrett Anderson, was a member of both the NUWSS and the WSPU, and several prominent campaigners veered from one to the other. Sylvia Pankhurst broke away from her mother and sister to form the East London Federation of Suffragettes in 1914. Princess Sophia Duleep Singh was a member of the

WSPU but also prominent in the Women's Tax Resistance League. Kate Parry Frye, actress and daughter of a Liberal MP, marched in processions with both the NUWSS and the Actresses' Franchise League, was a member of the WSPU, and was then employed for several years as an organiser for the New Constitutional Society for Women's Suffrage.

THE FIRST WORLD WAR

The outbreak of war in 1914 had a devastating impact on many working women. Food prices soared, male breadwinners went off to fight, and businesses collapsed in areas such as dressmaking. Some suffrage organisations shifted their focus onto relieving distress, by raising funds and setting up workshops to help unemployed women earn money. As the war continued, women began to abandon some traditional female areas of work such as domestic service, and instead took jobs previously undertaken by men in factories, offices, transport, agriculture, policing and munitions work. This was accelerated by the introduction of conscription in 1916 when many more women came into the workforce in the Home Front to free men for active service. Such work often involved long hours in dangerous working conditions, especially in munitions factories.

In itself, the war caused both the House of Commons and House of Lords to employ women in roles other than cleaning and catering for the first time. The Commons employed four "Girl Porters" from April 1917 until male staff returned from the Great War in March 1919. They were Elsie and Mabel Clark (aged

Right
Press cutting showing
Marion Wallace-Dunlop's
protest in Parliament, June
1909. The note says that
the photograph was faked

Below
The NUWSS "Tree", 1913.
The acorn indicates the
formation of the first
suffrage societies in 1867

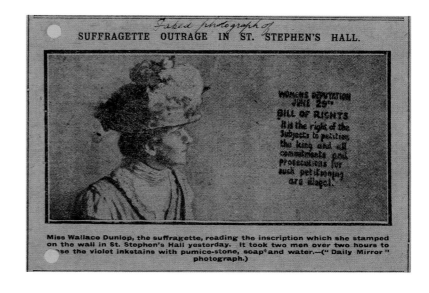

16 and 14), Vera Goldsmith (age 16) and Dorothy Hart (age 18). The Serjeant-at-Arms was initially very worried by this "innovation", but by the time they left he wrote, "It is impossible for me to speak too highly of the way these girls have done their work, and their conduct has been exemplary throughout." Meanwhile, the Lords employed May Court and Mabel Waterman as clerical assistants from April 1918. Court, whose twin brother Robert had previously worked in the Lords' Accounts department before being killed in action, went on to become Accountant and head of department, retiring in 1944 after 26 years' service in the House of Lords.

All suffragette prisoners were released at the beginning of the War. Women worked on the front lines as doctors, nurses and ambulance drivers. Suffrage campaigners in these roles included Elsie Inglis, who set up the Scottish Women's Hospitals for Foreign Service; and Louisa Garrett Anderson and Flora Murray, who established military hospitals including the all-female-staffed Endell Street Military Hospital in London. Nurses included Princess Sophia Duleep Singh for the Red Cross, who tended wounded Indian soldiers in Brighton. Women served in the Women's Auxiliary Army Corps from 1916, the Women's Royal Navy from 1917, and the Women's Royal Air Force from 1918. Suffrage leaders were divided in their attitude to the Great War. Emmeline and Christabel Pankhurst suspended the WSPU's militant campaigning and put their energies into helping mobilise women for war work, motivated by strong patriotism as well as a belief that this would help women secure the vote after the war. In contrast, Sylvia Pankhurst opposed the war as a pacifist. She initially worked to alleviate the poverty of women in the East End at the outbreak of war, and later campaigned against conscription and for the peace effort. Charlotte Despard, another socialist and pacifist, also campaigned for peace even though her brother, Sir John French, was commander-in-chief of the British Expeditionary Force. Over in Australia, Adela Pankhurst became a leading speaker for the Women's Peace Army.

The leadership of the National Union of Women's Suffrage Societies split over the war. Millicent Fawcett chose to support the war effort. Others, including Catherine Marshall, Chrystal Macmillan and Kathleen Courtney, resigned in protest, believing that international peace and women's rights were interlinked. Macmillan, Courtney and Emmeline Pethick Lawrence were the only three British attendees at the Women's International Congress in The Hague in 1915; Marshall and others helped plan the event but were barred from travelling by the British government. The Congress led to the formation of the Women's International League for Peace and Freedom.

The war affected other suffrage campaigners in different ways. In 1915 former WSPU activist Margaret Haig Thomas (later Viscountess Rhondda) was returning from a business trip to the USA with her father on the *Lusitania* when it was torpedoed. She spent hours in the freezing water before being rescued. She went on to help mobilise women for the war effort in Wales and nationally, emerging as a great feminist leader after the war. The suffragist Eleanor Rathbone worked in Liverpool organising separation allowances to support wives of soldiers and sailors, which led her to develop her later thinking on family allowances.

THE REPRESENTATION OF THE PEOPLE ACT

The suffrage campaign continued throughout the war. Breakaway groups such as the "Suffragettes of the WPSU", led by Rose Lamartine Yates, continued to advocate militant tactics after Emmeline and Christabel Pankhurst abandoned them, and the Women's Freedom League never stopped actively campaigning. It was clear that there had been a significant shift in public opinion in favour of woman's suffrage since the beginning of the war, and even Asquith accepted in August 1916 that change was inevitable. Nevertheless, the behind-the-scenes lobbying of Millicent Fawcett and Eleanor Rathbone was crucial in ensuring that votes for women were considered alongside men in the Speaker's Conference on Electoral Reform convened that year, and that the Conference recommendations were implemented.

The origins of the Speaker's Conference lay in an urgent need for technical changes to electoral registration for any election after the War; but it quickly became a vehicle for long-debated reforms, including the enfranchisement of the approximately 40 per cent of men not entitled to vote because of the residential and property qualifications required. A cross-party conference of 32 MPs and peers, chaired by James Lowther, Speaker of the House of Commons, was set up in October 1916 to discuss the extent of reform required. The conference considered franchise reform, the redistribution of seats, electoral registration and the method and cost of elections. It included some long-standing supporters of women's suffrage such as Willoughby Dickinson and Sir John Simon, as well as some dedicated opponents such as Frederick Banbury. In January 1917 the conference recommended by a majority that the vote be given to women on the local government register, or whose husbands were on it, provided they had reached a specified age "of which 30 and 35 received most favour".

The Representation of the People bill introduced later in 1917 embodied the recommendations of the Speaker's Conference. Although there was still strong residual opposition in Parliament, the crucial divisions on women's suffrage were passed decisively, with 385 votes to 55 in the Commons, and 134 votes to 71 in the Lords.

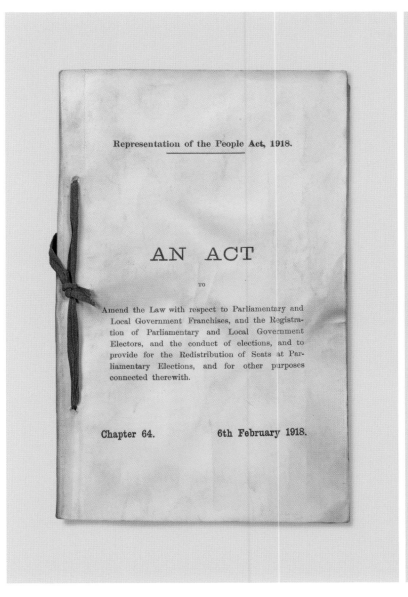

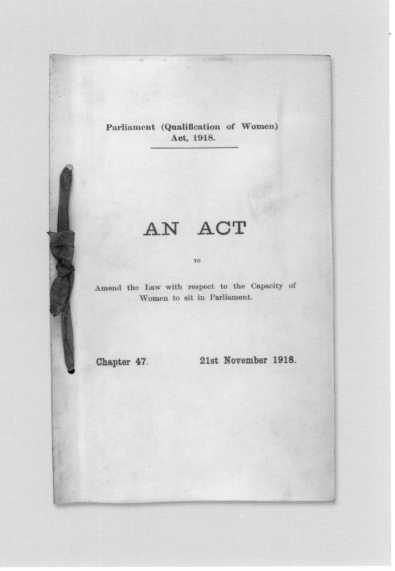

Above, left
Representation of the People Act, 1918,
the Act that allowed virtually all men and
the first women to vote in Parliamentary
elections for the first time

Above, right
Parliament (Qualification of
Women) Act, 1918, the Act
that allowed women to stand
for election to Parliament

"I would never take an oath of allegiance to the power I meant to overthrow"

Constance Markievicz

Labour and Irish Nationalist MPs unanimously voted in favour, with significant reversals among both Liberal and Conservative MPs who had opposed before the war.

As passed, the Representation of the People Act 1918 allowed nearly 13 million men and eight and a half million women to vote. All men over the age of 21 were given the vote, apart from conscientious objectors who were disqualified for five years. Men on military or naval service connected with the current war could vote from the age of 19. The vote was given to women over the age of 30 who qualified for the local government franchise, meaning they had to occupy either a dwelling-house of any value, or land or premises of a yearly value of not less than five pounds. Women were also enabled to vote under the university franchise on the same basis as men, providing they were 30 years old. In practice, the age limit meant that no young women war workers could vote, even if they were serving in the armed forces or working in a munitions factory. The property qualification additionally disenfranchised women over 30 who lived at home with parents or other family members, or in furnished rooms or hostels, even though many such women were likely to have been supporting the war effort working in factories, shops and offices. Domestic staff living in their employer's house were also excluded.

The age and property restrictions were designed to ensure women did not form the majority of the electorate, as they would otherwise have done because of the loss of men in the war. Overall the provisos placed on the women's vote left unenfranchised approximately one third of the adult female population. Approximately one third of those excluded were over 30. Gender equality and rewarding war service were not as important principles of reform as the retention of traditional considerations of electoral eligibility, such as age, respectability, class, property and education.

Once some women had the vote, attention immediately turned to the question of whether women could become MPs. Women were barred from standing as Parliamentary candidates by common law, not statute law, which meant that it would be a matter for individual returning officers in constituencies as to whether to accept female candidates or not – a recipe for chaos. Following a test case by Nina Boyle from the Women's Freedom League, a resolution to correct the situation was brought to the House of Commons by Liberal MP Herbert Samuel in October 1918, and overwhelmingly passed. The Parliament (Qualification of Women) Act 1918 was subsequently rushed through both Houses just in time before the end of the Parliamentary session, and allowed women to stand for election to the House of Commons in the General Election of December 1918. The Act qualified women aged 21 and over to stand for Parliament – even though women under 30 were still not entitled to vote.

Seventeen women candidates stood, including former suffragette Christabel Pankhurst for the Women's Party. Constance Markievicz was the only one elected. Markievicz had been active in the cause of women's suffrage, Irish nationalism, socialism and trade unionism. A member of the Irish Republican party, Sinn Féin, she had been convicted of treason for her part in the Easter Rising in 1916. Though released from prison in an amnesty in 1917, she was imprisoned again as a result of alleged collusion with the Germans in 1918, and fought the election from a cell in Holloway Prison. Like other Sinn Féin party members who were elected, she did not take her seat in Westminster. Technically, her election may have been invalid as a result of her conviction and her marriage to a foreign national, though the objection was not made at the time. She went on to take her seat as a member of the first Irish Parliament, the Dáil Éireann, and to play a significant role in Irish politics.

Right
Constance Markievicz
photographed on the
S. S. Aquitania in 1922

THE TOMB, 1918–63

In 1918, anticipating the arrival of women MPs, the Office of Works set up the first Lady Members' Room, "a gaunt room with large heavy oak tables and chairs, as forbidding as a Victorian school-marm." Nancy Astor was its first inhabitant following her election in 1919. She was joined in 1921 by Margaret Wintringham – a Liberal – and by the first Labour women in 1923. Ellen Wilkinson later described it as "Really rather like a tomb"; it was ill-ventilated, with too few desks, only one coat hook, the toilet placed at the farthest possible point from the room, and no bath.

Paula Bartley
Oonagh Gay
Helen McCarthy
Duncan Sutherland
Jacqui Turner

Previous pages
The introduction of Nancy Astor as the first woman Member of Parliament in 1919, by Charles Sims. Her supporters are David Lloyd George, the prime minister, to her left, and Arthur Balfour, the former prime minister, on her right

---

Above
"The Tomb": the first Lady Members' Room in Parliament, 1919

THE FIRST FEMALE MPS

The Lady Members' Room was re-located down the hallway to a slightly larger space in 1931, but was still inadequate for the slowly growing number of women MPs. Other facilities for the early women MPs, and also their female staff and visitors, were poor. Women were restricted from various areas such as dining rooms and galleries for many years. However, the Lady Members' Room did allow for some female camaraderie to develop in some circumstances. Shirley Williams recalled one occasion following a speech where, "I retreated to the Lady Members' Room where Margaret Thatcher was ironing a dress. 'You did well,' she said. 'After all, we can't let them get the better of us'."

In her 1926 pamphlet *What The Vote Has Done*, Millicent Fawcett championed the Act that had made it "possible for a constituency to choose a woman as its representative in the House of Commons". Few women, however, stood for election throughout the 1920s, and even fewer succeeded. Despite their small number, the presence of women in the House reminded politicians of the importance of the female electorate and served as a stimulus for progressive legislation. The election of women brought political attention to their needs, and to issues related to the home and family.

The work of the first cohort of female MPs has often been overshadowed by the pre-war feminist movement and suffrage campaigns that got them there, but the contribution and significant achievements made by women both inside and outside of parliament affirms their political influence. Twenty-one female MPs trickled into parliament between 1919 and 1931. In this early period there were distinctly different types of female politician. The majority of Conservative and Liberal women MPs succeeded to their husbands' seats or were muscled into

a constituency by aristocratic or well-connected families via carefully controlled by-elections. Of the 21, seven were elected to their husbands' seats and a further three were heavily sponsored by their husbands or families. By contrast, the mostly unmarried Labour MPs had strong local government, feminist or trade union backgrounds and were elected in greater numbers at general elections.

The first female actually to sit in the chamber of House of Commons was the American divorcee, Nancy Astor. In 1919, she replaced her second husband, Waldorf Astor, as the Conservative MP for Plymouth Sutton after he inherited a peerage and became a member of the House of Lords. She won the resulting by-election with more votes than the Labour and Liberal candidates combined. Nancy's time in the Commons was initially intended to be temporary, as her husband intended to extricate himself from the Lords and return to the Commons. In fact, he never did and she remained in the Commons until 1945.

Suffrage campaigners were initially dismayed that the first woman MP to take her seat was so much a product of the political establishment. To many her proximity to her husband made her an acceptable candidate; to some it negated the work that the Votes for Women campaign had achieved. Nevertheless, Astor's introduction to the Commons was an indication of how much a challenge for the political establishment the arrival of women would be. The presence of a woman had an immediate impact on parliamentary etiquette and procedure: the Speaker, James Lowther, wondered how to address the "Gentlemen of the House" and if he should allow her to keep her hat on when speaking.

Despite her position Astor had to cope with a constant and insidious sexism that undermined

Right
Nancy, Viscountess
Astor (1879–1964), MP
for Plymouth 1919–45,
by Zsigmond Kisfaludi
Strobl, 1933

NANCY ASTOR, M.P.

3, Elliot Terrace,
Plymouth.

November 25th, 1922.

Dear Madam,

    I am very sorry indeed that I was not able to thank personally all those who came forward to help me at the election. They are so many that it would have been impossible to see them all before I left Plymouth. But I want to send you my most grateful thanks for your own share in the victory. I realise that the splendid majority obtained, is largely due to the loyalty and hard work of those who like yourself rallied round me during the election campaign. I appreciate deeply this proof of your confidence in me and I will try to do all I can to be worthy of it, by working to the best of my ability for the welfare of Plymouth and of our country. I shall never forget the whole-hearted support and the devoted service given by so many in the division.

Yours sincerely,

Nancy Astor

3, ELLIOT TERRACE,
THE HOE,
PLYMOUTH.

15th Novr. 1919.

Dear Mrs Le Cras,

    I was more than touched by your charming present last night, and thank you once more for your splendid work which I must thank you for personally, but we are all realizing that it is really for the country. Again thank you so much for the beautiful flowers.

Yours Sincerely,

Nancy Astor

It has been a
fight — but for
the right

Mrs. P.B. Le Cras,
58, Ebrington Street,
PLYMOUTH.

Mrs. Le Cras,
58, Ebrington Street,
Plymouth.

N.A.
4, ST JAMES' SQUARE,
S.W.1.

LWJ.
    5th Dec., 1919.

Dear Mrs. Le Cras,

    Many thanks for your letter, and for the suggestion as to the Primrose League meeting. You cannot tell how much I appreciate all you are doing to help me in my difficult task.

Yours sincerely,

Nancy Astor

58, Ebrington Street,
Plymouth.

It is a Task too —

Parliamentary Borough of Plymouth.

SUTTON DIVISION.

NOVEMBER, 1919.

Please admit Mrs. Le Cras
at the Counting of the Votes in the Guildhall, at
10·45 a.m., on Friday, the 28th November, 1919.

Please Produce this Card

Acting Returning Officer.

COUNTING AGENT.

TOWN CLERK'S OFFICE,
PLYMOUTH
November, 1919.

PARLIAMENTARY ELECTION.

SUTTON DIVISION.

Madam,

    You having been appointed an Agent by The Viscountess Astor to attend on her behalf at the Counting of the Votes at the Guildhall, on Friday, the 28th instant at 11 a.m., it is necessary that you should make a Declaration of Secrecy before the commencement of the Poll.

    I enclose a Form of Declaration which should be made before any Justice of the Peace for the Borough and returned to me **before the opening of the Poll on Saturday next.**

    I am, Sir,
Yours obediently,

Mrs. Le Cras   ACTING RETURNING OFFICER.

THE SUTTON ELECTION.

Lady Astor First English Woman M.P.

BIG MAJORITY.

VISCOUNTESS ASTOR	14,495
Mr. W. T. GAY	9,292
Mr. I. FOOT	4,139

This is to certify that
Mrs. Le Cras was the first
lady to vote at the Grey Coat
School.

E. H. Ralph   14⅕ /18.

SUTTON DIVISION PARLIAMENTARY BYE-ELECTION, 1919.

Lady Astor's Central Committee Room.

ELECTION AGENT
C. G. BRIGGS.

'PHONE
PLYMOUTH 203
TELEGRAMS
UNIONIST, PLYMOUTH

17, LOCKYER STREET,
PLYMOUTH.

Nov 11/19

Dear Mrs Le Cras

    The Bearer is a friend of ours from Rugby & is anxious to obtain some information re Co. op. movement.

Will you please assist him?

Yours faithfully
C. G. Briggs

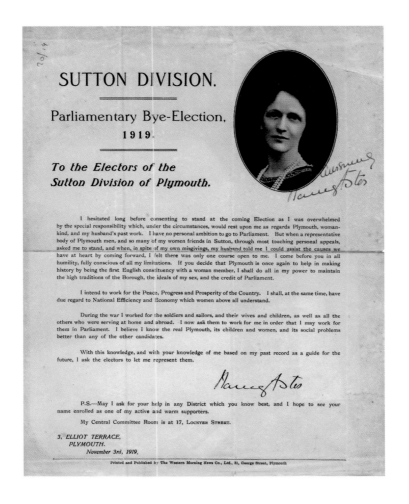

SUTTON DIVISION.

Parliamentary Bye-Election,
1919.

To the Electors of the
Sutton Division of Plymouth.

I hesitated long before consenting to stand at the coming Election as I was overwhelmed by the special responsibility which, under the circumstances, would rest upon me as regards Plymouth, woman-kind, and my husband's past work. I have no personal ambition to go to Parliament. But when a representative body of Plymouth men, and so many of my women friends in Sutton, through most touching personal appeals, asked me to stand, and when, in spite of my own misgivings, my husband told me I could assist the causes we have at heart by coming forward, I felt there was only one course open to me. I come before you in all humility, fully conscious of all my limitations. If you decide that Plymouth is once again to help in making history by being the first English constituency with a woman member, I shall do all in my power to maintain the high traditions of the Borough, the ideals of my sex, and the credit of Parliament.

I intend to work for the Peace, Progress and Prosperity of the Country. I shall, at the same time, have due regard to National Efficiency and Economy which women above all understand.

During the war I worked for the soldiers and sailors, and their wives and children, as well as all the others who were serving at home and abroad. I now ask them to work for me in order that I may work for them in Parliament. I believe I know the real Plymouth, its children and women, and its social problems better than any of the other candidates.

With this knowledge, and with your knowledge of me based on my past record as a guide for the future, I ask the electors to let me represent them.

P.S.—May I ask for your help in any District which you know best, and I hope to see your name enrolled as one of my active and warm supporters.

My Central Committee Room is at 17, Lockyer Street.

3, ELLIOT TERRACE,
PLYMOUTH.
November 3rd, 1919.

Printed and Published by The Western Morning News Co., Ltd., 31, George Street, Plymouth

Opposite
Items relating to Nancy Astor's by-election campaign in Plymouth Sutton, 1919. They were collected by Bessie Le Cras, one of the earliest female election agents. Her work included helping manage the election campaign and assisting the party constituency organisation

Above
Astor's first election campaign leaflet, November 1919

her attempts to be taken seriously. She prevented comments on her clothing by adopting a uniform of dark jacket and skirt, white blouse and tricorn hat which set the style for her feminine colleagues in years to come. She took on a culture of misogyny and often outright resentment as she spent almost two years as the only woman in the House of Commons. She delivered her maiden speech on 24 February 1920 before an audience of over 500 male MPs, many of them hostile. Her speech, reflecting her abstentionist politics, was on the need for restrictions on the sale of alcohol: she commented that it took "a bit of courage to address the House on that vexed question, drink". Consistently aware that she was representing her sex as well as her constituency, she claimed: "to speak for hundreds of women and children throughout the country who cannot speak for themselves". In 1923, she was responsible for the first bill introduced by a woman to be passed into law, the Intoxicating Liquor (Sale to Persons under Eighteen) Bill.

The Commons never grew to love Astor. Her enemies dubbed her "Lady Dis-Astor". She was unable, or unwilling, to cultivate a parliamentary manner, and while the many Astor anecdotes have an eccentric charm, her colleagues grew irritated by her constant interruptions and audible commentaries on others' speeches. Astor was "an unconventional MP". She admitted herself that she was more of a "nuisance" than a "force" in the Commons, in part because she lacked any political philosophy. She was however, a vociferous advocate of equal voting rights and she supported welfare reforms and access to the professions for women. She helped to spare the women's section of the Metropolitan Police from the "Geddes Axe" (the 1920s cuts in public expenditure). She encouraged other female MPs regardless of political party, including the second woman MP, Margaret Wintringham, elected in 1921 as a Liberal, replacing her husband on his death. She struck up often unlikely friendships with each new intake of women, including "Red" Ellen Wilkinson, the Labour MP for Middlesbrough East elected in 1924. Astor believed that the support of women was the reason she stayed in Parliament; but entering it had been a different matter: "Now I realise it was a jolly good thing that I was the first woman, for the first person, I knew nearly everybody in London, I knew many people in the House of Commons, I was connected with a priest, intimate friends with the editor of *The Times*, owning *The Observer*, and I really cared about social reform and I cared what I was there for and I had money enough to get good secretaries. It wasn't so much what I was but I had so much to keep me up." Ultimately, Astor was a greater success as a cause than as an individual MP. Her enduring significance was secured the moment she swore the oath.

Amongst the causes Astor was most passionate in supporting was equal franchise, giving women the vote on the same terms as men (to women under the age of 30 and without property qualifications). Women's suffrage organisations continued to campaign on this issue after 1918, and it was the subject of many private members' bills and Parliamentary questions between 1919 and 1927. The House of Commons passed a bill in favour of equal franchise as early as 1919 but the government was not willing to support it. Many Conservative MPs, including Winston Churchill, feared the effect that equal franchise would have on their party, and the *Daily Mail* whipped up a tabloid campaign against the "flapper vote". But, following personal statements in favour of equal

Above
Susan Lawrence leading
a demonstration on
equal franchise, c. 1920.
Lawrence later became
one of the first Labour
women MPs

by an acute awareness of class-based injustice. Ellen Wilkinson wrote in the suffragette journal *The Vote* that "the woman who earns her living, whether as a wife or a wage earner... is suffering mainly from the wrongs that afflict all her class". She described herself as a "flaming socialist". Similarly, Jennie Lee, brought up by working class and socialist parents, expressed a fiery determination to change the fortunes of her class.

THE 1930S

When in 1936 Eleanor Rathbone reflected upon the impact which women MPs had already made – and might make in the future – on British political life she played down the extent to which they were distinctive: "Those who expect women's contribution to be... utterly different from the contribution of men, will be disappointed," she wrote. "Perhaps five-sixths or nine-tenths of that contribution will be a fair sample of the whole mixed bag of parliamentary effort." Women, she argued, were formed politically in same way as men, through the "interacting forces of heredity, education, social environment, party politics, the nature of the constituency and its interests". It was fanciful to suppose that all women MPs would behave in an identical manner, favour the same causes and speak at all times with a united voice. Nevertheless, she accepted that the remainder of their contribution would be based on their unique perspective as women: "It is unquestionable that their differences in function, especially the difference between the paternal and the maternal function and all its results upon social life and occupational groupings, do bring it about that each sex tends to acquire a special kind of experience and to develop its own forms of expertise."

During the 1930s the expectation that women MPs would represent not only their constituents, but the interests of their sex, was widely held. But Rathbone's prediction that only a small portion of women's political energies would be channelled in this direction was proved correct. On occasion, women MPs forged cross-party solidarities and platforms for joint action, but most of the time they toed party lines or pursued political agendas unrelated to their shared status as women. Furthermore, women's capacity to effect change in Parliament was constrained by the fact of their being vastly outnumbered by men, and by the trivialising treatment they received from the interwar popular press.

Rathbone's own parliamentary career offers an illuminating example of what women MPs could achieve individually and the circumstances under which they could act collectively in the 1930s. An avowed feminist who disliked partisanship, Rathbone won election in 1929 as Independent Member for the Combined

franchise by Prime Minister Stanley Baldwin and his Home Secretary William Joynson Hicks, a Conservative government finally passed the Equal Franchise Act in 1928, with "just ten men" voting against it in the House of Commons. The Equal Franchise Act was one of a host of Acts passed during the 1920s affecting women's lives and gender equality. They also included the Sex Disqualification (Removal) Act 1919 that allowed women to enter certain professions for the first time including law, and legislation on property inheritance, nurses registration, marriage and divorce, equal guardianship, widows' and orphans' pensions, and adoption.

Women had been able to join the Labour party on the same terms as men since its inception and the party had put women at the heart of their 1918 manifesto. At the "Flapper Election" of 1929 following the Equal Franchise Act, of the 14 women then elected, nine were Labour. Most of this first cohort of Labour women were from working-class backgrounds, and were motivated

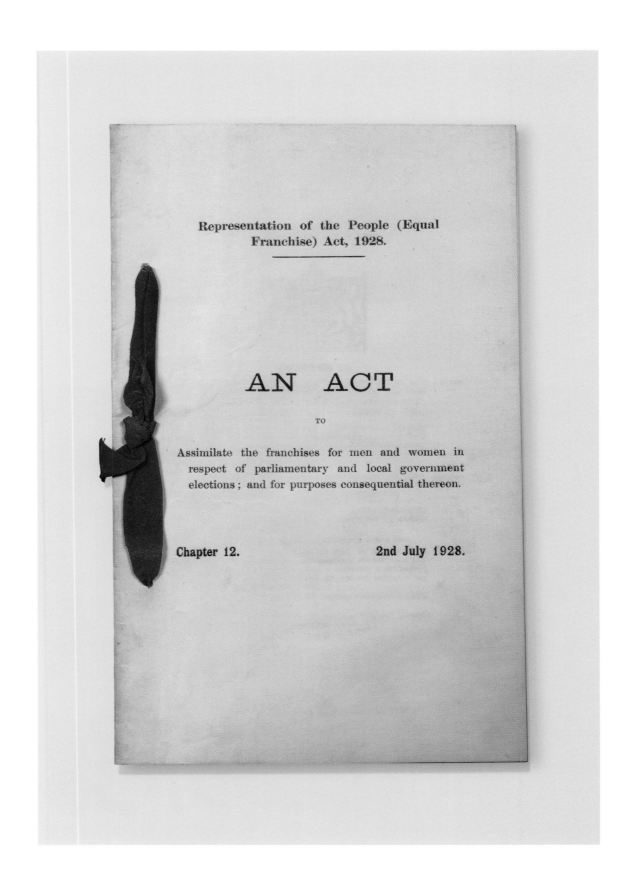

Right
Equal Franchise Act, 1928,
the Act that gave women
the vote on the same
terms as men, at age 21
and without any property
qualifications

English Universities, one of a small number of seats still returned by separate university electorates. She was a campaigning MP who ploughed her energies into promoting reforms which would help women, especially poorer mothers who were economically dependent on men. Rathbone's advocacy of Family Allowances, which were finally introduced in 1945, was one result. In the later 1930s, she also became a key voice in foreign-policy debates, vocally opposing the National Government's policy of appeasement and championing the cause of refugees seeking safe haven in Britain.

In her radicalism both on the domestic front and in international affairs, Rathbone found common cause with other women MPs. She helped to facilitate coordinated action in opposing the withdrawal of unemployment benefits to married women in 1931; in reforming the law which forced women to give up their nationality upon marriage to a foreign national; and in demanding equal pay for women civil servants. The first of these campaigns was unsuccessful, but the latter two demands were achieved in 1948 and 1955 respectively. As a critic of foreign policy, Rathbone forged an especially strong partnership with two other notable female parliamentarians of the decade, Labour's Ellen Wilkinson and the Conservative member for Kinross and

West Perthshire, the Duchess of Atholl. The trio made a well-publicised trip to war-torn Spain in 1937, drawing attention to the suffering of General Franco's victims and to the consequences of the British government's support for the policy of non-intervention.

In other areas, party loyalties and ideological differences could not be set aside so readily. Despite her best efforts, Nancy Astor's attempt to create a women's bloc in Parliament in 1929 foundered. Most women members chose instead to cultivate careers as faithful party supporters or as cause-driven campaigners – or to walk a tightrope in trying to balance the two. They did so from a position of numerical weakness. The pre-1945 highpoint for women's parliamentary representation was reached immediately after the 1931 election, when 15 female candidates were returned, accounting for a mere 2.4 per cent of the total number of MPs (though the election was a disaster for the female MPs of the Labour party, who all lost their seats). Nor were great strides made at ministerial level. Britain's first female Cabinet minister, Margaret Bondfield, who had been appointed Minister of Labour in 1929, lost her post with the fall of the second Labour government in the summer of 1931. There were to be no more women ministers until Florence Horsbrugh's appointment as parliamentary

Left
Women Labour MPs,
1929. Margaret Bondfield,
the first woman Cabinet
Minister, is centre front

secretary at the Ministry of Health in late 1939. Women were thus still very much newcomers in the masculine world of Westminster. Labour's Edith Summerskill described the atmosphere in Parliament as akin to that of "a boys' school which had decided to take a few girls".

This marginal status was compounded by a tabloid press which treated women MPs as novelty items by running endless stories about their sartorial choices and personal lives – coverage of a kind rarely experienced by male politicians. Some women found ways to make this media interest serve their own purposes. Ellen Wilkinson, for example, took full advantage of the cameras and reporters who accompanied her as she marched with the unemployed men of Jarrow from north-east England to Parliament in 1936. Wilkinson

knew that the spectacle of a diminutive redhead flanked by flat-capped male workers would grab headlines and help to raise public awareness of the continuing problems of unemployment. Nonetheless, taken as a whole, women MPs struggled to convince the press to report their political views and activities seriously in the 1930s. The obsession with dress, appearance and "human interest" was an ominous foretaste of what subsequent generations of female politicians would be forced to tolerate when dealing with the media.

The 1930s was, then, a decade of limited progress for women in Parliament, notwithstanding the distinguished contributions made by individuals such as Rathbone or Wilkinson. The fullest expression of what women could achieve collectively as legislators

– that distinctive element identified by Rathbone
– would have to wait until their representation in
Parliament came much closer to approaching a critical
mass. It was to be a long wait.

THE IMPACT OF THE WAR

With the outbreak of the Second World War,
Westminster was put on a war footing. Extraordinarily,
more than 40 women worked in a munitions factory in
the heart of Parliament under Central Lobby. They were
mostly Parliamentary staff and wives of MPs working on

a voluntary basis, plus some paid staff. Other women
participated in activities such as firewatching and Red
Cross nursing. Six became auxiliaries in the Palace of
Westminster Home Guard. The war saw increased
employment opportunities for a few women. Kay
Midwinter was appointed the first woman clerk (a
senior official, organising the procedure of the House
and its committees) in the House of Commons, working
for the National Expenditure Committee. She
went on to work for the Foreign Office and then the
United Nations after the war. Two other women were
employed as committee clerks on a temporary basis.
Jean Winder was appointed the first permanent female
Hansard reporter, fighting a long battle for equal pay
before retiring in 1960.

In 1940 Edith Summerskill helped to form the
Women for Westminster group to encourage more
women to stand for Parliament. The group urged
women party activists, whatever their political
affiliation, to support female candidates. Its creation
recognised the still negligible numbers of women in the
Commons. At the outbreak of the Second World War
there were 628 men MPs and a mere 12 women. Six
of the 12 were Conservatives: Nancy Astor, Florence
Horsburgh, Thelma Cazalet-Keir, Frances Davidson
(Viscountess Davidson), Mavis Tate, and Irene Ward.
Four were Labour: Ellen Wilkinson, Jennie Adamson,
Agnes Hardie and Edith Summerskill. There was one
Liberal, Megan Lloyd-George, and one Independent,
Eleanor Rathbone. They were later joined by two
widows, Beatrice Rathbone and Violet, Lady Apsley,
who replaced husbands killed on active service. Beatrice
Rathbone (whose husband was Eleanor's nephew)
married again, changed her name to Mrs Wright and
in 1943 became the first sitting woman MP to have a
baby. Lady Apsley was the first woman MP who was
a permanent wheelchair user.

This small group of women played a significant
part in domestic politics. Three of them – Nancy
Astor, Mavis Tate and Ellen Wilkinson – were said to
have played a role in forcing the vote that toppled
Neville Chamberlain as Prime Minister in May
1940. When Winston Churchill succeeded him, he
appointed Wilkinson and Florence Horsburgh to
ministerial posts. Both women were key figures in civil
defence. Horsburgh, as a Parliamentary Secretary
in the Ministry of Health, helped to organise the
evacuation of one and half million women and

Parliamentary Election
1931

Mrs. RUNGE, O.B.E.
for ROTHERHITHE

ROTHERHITHE LIBERAL AND MRS. RUNGE
Takes the Chair at Her Final Election Rally

Mr R. J. Winter, chairman of the Rotherhithe Liberal Association, was in the chair at the final rally of Mrs. N. Runge, the Rotherhithe National Conservative candidate, at Rotherhithe Town Hall on Saturday.

"I am on this platform supporting Mrs. Runge because when the country is faced with a crisis we should place the interests of the nation before party politics," he declared.

"This is no time for one party to fight against another. We must all pull together in the common cause, and it is for that reason that I appeal to you to send Mrs. Runge to Parliament as your representative."

Mrs. Runge had to deal with a number of hecklers and on several occasions she was interrupted by cries of "Good old Ben," and "Ben's got you beat." Mrs. Runge refused to be shouted down and continued her speech.

Mrs. Runge, Conservative candidate for Bermondsey, polling the first vote at seven in the morning. She carried a horseshoe for luck.

At Rotherhithe Mrs. Runge overcame a Socialist majority of over 10,000. Equally striking was the change over in three of Camberwell's four divisions—from a triple Socialist majority of nearly 16,000 to a triple Conservative majority of nearly 18,000.

Mrs. Norah Runge, Rotherhithe.

Let us hope that the House will find a new vital quality in the Idas, Thelmas, Irenes, Norahs, and whatnots.
They ought to strike a new note.

Mrs. Norah Runge, the victor at Rotherhithe, is an O.B.E. This order she gained for superintending the free buffet for soldiers and sailors at Paddington station during the war.

13 WOMEN M.P.s THIS TIME
All the Socialists Gone—Nine New Members

There are thirteen women M.P.s in the new Parliament—and of these no fewer than nine will take their seats in the House for the first time.

They will replace nine well-known women Socialists who have reaped a full share of the Labour Party rout.

In the 1924 Parliament there were only eight women and in the last fifteen.

Here are the successes and defeats:—

NEW WOMEN M.P.s
*Duchess of Atholl (C.), Perth and Kinross.
*Lady Astor (C.), Plymouth (Sutton).
*Miss Megan Lloyd George (L.), Anglesey.
*Lady Iveagh (C.), Southend-on-Sea.
Mrs. Helen Shaw (C.), Lanark (Bothwell).
Mrs. Ida Copeland (C.), Stoke-on-Trent.
Miss Thelma Cazalet (C.), East Islington.
Miss F. M. Graves (C.), Hackney South.
Miss F. Horsbrugh (C.), Dundee.
Hon. Mary Pickford (C.), Hammersmith.
Mrs. N. Runge (C.), Rotherhithe.
Mrs. H. B. Tate (C.), West Willesden.
Miss Irene Ward (C.), Wallsend.
  * Indicates re-election.

WOMEN M.P.s DEFEATED
Miss Jennie Lee (S.), N. Lanark.
Lady Noel-Buxton (S.), Norwich N.
Dr. Marion Philips (S.), Sunderland.
Mrs. Leah Manning (S.), E. Islington.
Miss Margaret Bondfield (S.), Wallsend.
Miss Susan Lawrence (S.), East Ham North.
Mrs. Mary Hamilton (S.), Blackburn.
Miss Ellen Wilkinson (S.), Middlesbrough East.
Miss E. Picton-Turbervill (S.), The Wrekin.

Mrs. Helen Shaw won Bothwell (Lanarkshire) from the Socialist man member and secured a turnover of more than 6,000.

Mrs. Ida Copeland is the wife of a pottery manufacturer.

Miss Thelma Cazalet, the Empire candidate, wrested East Islington from the present member, Mrs. Leah Manning, the president of the National Union of Teachers.

Miss F. M. Graves beat Mr. Herbert Morrison, ex-Minister of Transport. Daughter of a Sussex alderman, formerly attached War Office and acted as liaison officer between the War Office and the League of Nations at the Peace Conference in 1919.

Miss F. Horsbrugh for her war services was made a member of the British Empire Order.

LORD STERNDALE'S DAUGHTER
Hon. Mary Pickford, daughter of Lord Sterndale, a former Master of the Rolls. Received C.B.E. in 1929 for national and political services.

Mrs. N. Runge (C.), Rotherhithe, London social worker. Acted as superintendent of the soldiers' and sailors' day and night free buffet at Paddington Station during the war.

Mrs. H. B. Tate (C.), West Willesden. A cousin of Lord Hailsham.

Miss Irene Ward. For four years took leading part in administration of Newcastle Food Office, an hon. secretary of Central Newcastle Conservative Association, and made a C.B.E. in 1924. She beat Miss Bondfield in her Wallsend stronghold by a majority of 7,000.

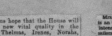

WOMEN M.P.s

MISS FLORENCE HORSBURGH (DUNDEE), MRS. N. C. RUNGE (ROTHERHITHE), MISS THELMA CAZALET (EAST Islington), Mrs. Ida Copeland (Stoke), Hon. Mary Pickford (N. Hammersmith), Mrs. H. B. Tate (West Willesden), Lady Iveagh (Southend).

Above

Scrapbooks of Norah Runge MP, 1931–1935. Runge was Conservative MP for Rotherhithe, east London. Her speeches in Parliament reflect concern for the poor in her constituency, slum clearance, and a strike by Thames Lightermen. Her daughter Peg collected two scrapbooks of press cuttings concerned with her Parliamentary career

"Jarrow has passed through a period of industrial depression without parallel in the town's history"

Ellen Wilkinson

Opposite
Ellen Wilkinson addressing
a crowd of Jarrow Marchers
in Hyde Park following
their march from Jarrow to
London, 1 November 1936

Above

House of Commons 1940, by John Worsley, 1947. Two women are visible on the government's side of the House, including Astor, clearly identifiable by her outfit

children from the major cities to safer places in the country. Later, she organised the casualty services, set up hostels for those bombed out of their homes, assumed responsibility for health and sanitation in the shelters and helped draft the post-war National Health Scheme. Ellen Wilkinson as a Parliamentary Secretary in the Home Office took charge of shelter provision, recruited women as fire-watchers and supervised changes in fire-fighting. Both exhausted themselves touring the country; both were bombed out of their homes, each on two separate occasions.

Women MPs responded vigorously to the challenge presented by wartime employment and labour policies which patently disadvantaged women workers. In 1940 Nancy Astor encouraged women backbenchers to

form a Woman Power Committee (WPC) to lobby government over a range of issues which concerned women, particularly equal pay and working conditions. There were disagreements: Ellen Wilkinson feared that the largely middle-class WPC might try to take over the role of the trade unions in representing women workers, and wrote to the Minister of Labour Ernest Bevin asking him to ensure that this did not happen. Bevin tried to circumvent the committee by establishing in March 1941 a separate Women's Consultative Committee (WCC) including trade unionists as well as women MPs. He asked them to advise him on the recruitment and organisation of women workers. However, most Labour women MPs continued to collaborate with the WPC, and the Conservative Mavis Tate formed an Equal Pay Campaign Committee, consisting of women from both bodies.

In December 1941, the committees worked together to try to obtain a guarantee of equal pay in the National Service (No. 2) Bill, which made certain groups of women liable for conscription. Though they failed, they continued to draw attention to the issue. In 1944 the Conservative MP Thelma Cazalet-Keir introduced an amendment to RA Butler's Education Bill to give women teachers the same pay as men. Although the amendment was passed, the following day Churchill demanded a reversal of the vote, angrily treating the issue as a matter of confidence in the government. The amendment was overturned, with only two women – Edith Summerskill and Agnes Hardie – voting for equal pay. It was a major defeat for the feminist MPs and a great disappointment for Cazalet-Keir, forced to vote against her own amendment.

Women MPs collaborated to challenge other discriminatory laws, including the 1939 War Injuries Act, which had set women's compensation for war-related injuries at 33 per cent less than men's. In November 1942 Mavis Tate, seconded by Edith Summerskill, moved an amendment to the Act, arguing in her speech that "this is not a party issue. It is not an issue between the sexes. It is an issue that is confined to justice". Other women backbenchers voted for Tate's amendment but the two women ministers remained loyal to the government and voted against. Tate's amendment failed but the government accepted the injustice of the 1939 Act and set up a

Above

Women MPs celebrating
Megan Lloyd George's 20th
anniversary in Parliament,
31 May 1949

Select Committee on which five women MPs served.
On 7 April 1943 Parliament voted to accept its
recommendations of equal compensation.

At times, parliamentary debates on these issues
were characterised not so much as a clash between
the parties as a clash between male and female MPs.
There was wit and humour as well as seriousness.
When Mrs Tate was asked by a male MP whether
women ever made mistakes, she replied "I should be
the last woman in the world to pretend that women
do not make mistakes, when I look around and see
some of the men they bring into the world."

In 1945 Ellen Wilkinson and Florence Horsburgh
accompanied Clement Attlee, Anthony Eden and
Lord Halifax to the San Francisco conference that
established the United Nations. Following the end
of the war in Europe, the Coalition government
disbanded and was replaced by a Conservative
caretaker government. Churchill appointed Thelma
Cazalet-Keir Parliamentary Secretary in the Ministry
of Education but told her not to bother with her
"equal pay nonsense"; in what seemed like a gesture
of compensation, however, the government passed
Eleanor Rathbone's Family Allowance Act 1945.

There can be no doubt that women had been
essential to the war effort, in agriculture, in industry,
in civil defence, and in community welfare. Many
served with the uniformed services; large numbers
worked in factories; others worked as mechanics,
engineers, ambulance drivers, electricians and
plumbers. Some became secret agents working in
occupied Europe. And a very small number were MPs
who worked hard to protect women's interests even
in the face of government opposition. Nevertheless,

at the end of the war, as had happened at the end of
the First World War, many women were encouraged
to give up paid work and return to the home to take
care of their husbands and family.

THE 1945 ELECTION AND AFTER

The July 1945 election was a watershed for many
reasons. It had been ten years since the previous general
election (there was no election during the war) and the
war had produced huge changes in government and
society and new policy challenges. The decisive result
of the 1945 election, a landslide for Labour, produced
the first Labour government with a secure majority and
mandate to introduce a welfare state. It also produced
a significant increase in the number of women in the
House. They included some of the most important
politicians in the post-war period.

Eighty-seven women stood as candidates, a 25 per
cent increase on 1935. Twenty-four women MPs were
elected, 15 of whom were new members. All but three
of the 24 were Labour. There was only one Conservative
(Viscountess Davidson), one Liberal (Megan Lloyd
George) and one Independent (Eleanor Rathbone). The
Conservative minister Florence Horsburgh lost her seat.
A by-election in 1946 brought in a second Conservative
woman, Priscilla, Lady Tweedsmuir. Some areas of the
UK elected a woman MP for the first time, including
Birmingham (Edith Wills), Liverpool (Bessie Braddock)
and Leeds (Alice Bacon). But after 1945 there was little
further progress in the number of women MPs: up to
1987 it did not increase beyond 29, representing under
five per cent of the House.

Three of the women re-elected in 1945, Ellen
Wilkinson, Edith Summerskill and Jennie Adamson,
were promoted immediately. Wilkinson, as Minister of
Education, became the second woman to hold Cabinet
rank. She died shortly after raising the school-leaving
age to 15 in April 1947. Summerskill was appointed a
junior minister in the Ministry of Food, dealing with
food rationing and continuing shortages. In 1949, she
sponsored the Milk (Special Designation) Bill, requiring
milk to be pasteurised against tuberculosis, so fulfilling
a long campaign begun by Astor and Wintringham in
the 1920s. As a doctor, Summerskill's parliamentary
interests also extended to women's health issues,
including childbirth and abortion. Adamson was

Above

Women MPs including Irene Ward, Barbara Castle and Dr Edith Summerskill outside the House of Commons with a petition of 80,000 signatures for equal pay, 8 March 1954

appointed a junior minister at the Ministry of Pensions, but she resigned as an MP in 1946 to become Deputy Chair of the Unemployment Assistance Board. Jennie Lee had to wait until 1964 for a substantial government post, when she became Minister for the Arts, and was charged with establishing what became known as the Open University. Megan Lloyd George, first elected in 1929, but emerging as a strong political force and radical voice in her own right following the death of her father, became Deputy Leader of the Liberal party in 1949.

Most of the new women MPs elected in 1945 had spent decades in the Labour or trades union movement, and knew each other. Some had sought selection for over a decade. They included journalist Barbara Ayrton-Gould, a former suffragette, imprisoned for window-smashing in 1912, and the barrister Freda Corbet. Nearly all, apart from Grace Colman, had been married. Most had families which had promoted political careers for daughters and wives, and many had trained as teachers. Jean Mann, a Glasgow MP with five children and a husband long unemployed, knew the realities of the poverty which she hoped the welfare state would eradicate. Many had been councillors, including Bessie Braddock, who had been prominent in local politics in Liverpool. Caroline Ganley and Mabel Ridealgh had long careers in the Co-operative Movement.

Labour women MPs were dedicated to the introduction of the welfare state and the implementation of their party manifesto, rather than pursuing an explicitly feminist agenda. They were vocal on the housing shortages, rationing and health needs of their constituents. Lucy Middleton, for example, served on the Estimates Committee and was influential on securing war damage payments. But many of the issues they pursued were of particular relevance to women. Leah Manning unsuccessfully pressed for family planning to be included within the NHS. Women continued to pursue equal pay and fought for an end to the married women's bar in the civil service and local government.

Three of the younger women MPs elected in 1945 – Barbara Castle, Alice Bacon and Margaret Herbison – would come to serve in the Labour governments of the 1960s and 1970s. In the 1945 Parliament, Castle became Parliamentary Private Secretary (PPS) to the Chancellor Stafford Cripps, an early indication of her abilities and ambition. She promoted the only successful private members' bill by a woman MP in this Parliament, the Criminal Law Amendment Bill of 1950, which gave women working as prostitutes more legal protection. As ever, the press were as ready to focus on her red hair and glamorous outfits as on her intellect. The Conservative Lady Tweedsmuir, who

Below

Margaret "Peggy" Herbison was Labour
MP for North Lanarkshire, 1945–70.
A collection of her papers and artefacts
were found in a Parliamentary desk in
2005, having apparently been abandoned
there in the 1950s. The papers reflect her
interests including Scotland, education,
women and the Labour Party

Above
Margaret Haig Thomas,
Viscountess Rhondda
(1883–1958), by Alice
Mary Burton, 1931

came into the House through a by-election in 1946, was – at 31 – the youngest woman MP, and attracted similar attention.

Women MPs progressed within party and parliamentary structures. Florence Paton became the first woman to join the Speaker's Panel of Members appointed to chair committees. In 1948 Viscountess Davidson became the first woman MP to be elected to the Conservative 1922 Committee Executive. In 1951, when Churchill returned as Prime Minister of a Conservative government, he appointed Florence Horsburgh – who had just regained a seat in the Commons – as Minister of Education; in 1953 he made it a Cabinet post, and Florence Horsburgh thus became the first woman to be a Conservative Cabinet Minister.

There were colourful interludes: Bessie Braddock lost a long-running libel case against the Bolton Evening News which had claimed she danced a jig on the floor of the House during the Transport Bill guillotine debates

in 1947. Braddock, a formidable presence, became in March 1952 the first woman to be named and suspended from a Commons sitting, following her protests about not being called to speak. Dame Irene Ward took an interest in developing female staff recruitment in the Commons, highlighting the lower pay offered to wartime female clerks: in 1955 she threatened to demonstrate how she was physically capable of carrying a library ladder into the Commons chamber if an advert specifying male-only librarians were not withdrawn; women had been employed in the Commons Library since 1946. Special legislation was passed in October 1945 to allow Jean Mann to retain her seat, when it emerged that her membership of a Scottish rent tribunal had inadvertently disqualified her as an MP.

And while women now held roles as senior party politicians and had national profiles, there were still cross-party friendships, promoted in part by the Lady Members' Room. In June 1949 Megan Lloyd George held a tea party for all women MPs to celebrate her 20 years in the House, and in her autobiography Leah Manning related visits with the Liberal MP to cinema matinees.

Progress had clearly been made. But the increase in the numbers of women elected to Parliament was not sustained: for 40 years after 1945 the number of women in the Commons hovered around the mid-twenties, or sometimes less, and women were still poorly represented in the Cabinet and even at junior ministerial level. It would take much more deliberate action to increase their numbers.

WOMEN IN THE HOUSE OF LORDS

The story of women's admission to the House of Lords is less well-known than that of the campaign for votes for women, but it is a remarkable one. It was not until 1963, 45 years after winning the vote, that women sat in both

"Probably this is the first occasion in 900 years that the voice of a woman has been heard in the deliberations of this House"

Baroness Elliot of Harwood

Houses of Parliament on equal terms with men. This is in contrast both to the House of Commons and other spheres such as the legal profession, which accepted women in the period around 1918. Indeed, for many men, it was partly these advances elsewhere which made it imperative to preserve the Lords as a male-only institution. But a more enduring obstacle than sexist attitudes was the question's entanglement with the difficult issue of overall reform of the Lords, then mainly made up of men who were there by virtue of their inherited peerage titles. The issue had been under debate since the reforms to the parliamentary franchise in the 19th century – and it remains far from completely resolved even now. After 1918 politicians debated whether women's admission to the House of Lords should precede or accompany the reform of the unelected chamber. It was the latter view that tended to prevail.

For centuries, women were able to hold peerages in certain circumstances, either by creation or by succession if there were no male heirs, although they lacked the political rights – especially the right to sit in the Lords – which usually accompanied a peerage. The status of female peers was rarely raised in the suffrage debates, partly as suffragists feared alienating moderate supporters by making additional demands. Twenty women held hereditary peerages in 1918. Their position became even more anomalous after ministers blocked efforts, made in the Commons and the Lords, to include them in the Parliament (Qualification of Women) Act.

The most politically active woman peer was former suffragette Margaret Haig Mackworth (née Thomas), Viscountess Rhondda, who inherited her father's peerage and business interests in 1918 and later founded The Six Point Group, a feminist campaigning organisation, and *Time and Tide*, a feminist, political and literary journal.

Viscountess Rhondda decided to seek admittance to the House of Lords, motivated by a desire mainly to establish the principle of equality rather than to sit. The 1919 Sex Disqualification (Removal) Act seemed to provide her with an opportunity. Although an amendment specifically covering the Lords had been rejected, the Act nonetheless proclaimed that persons would not be barred by sex or marriage "from the exercise of any public function", so she petitioned the Crown for a writ of summons to Parliament.

In 1922 the House of Lords' Committee for Privileges, and the Attorney General, agreed that she should receive a writ. Women celebrated this decision, but it caused concern in official quarters right up to the King: the Lords now faced the arrival of more than 20 women led by a formidable ex-suffragette. By contrast, there were still only two women MPs. No decision of the committee for privileges had been challenged since 1869; nevertheless, the Lord Chancellor, the former anti-suffragist Viscount Birkenhead, had her claim referred back to it for reconsideration. The committee was expanded with about 20 additional members, including Birkenhead. After heated debate it disallowed Rhondda's claim, concluding that the words "public function" did not include sitting in the Lords.

These manoeuvrings angered women's groups, and Lady Rhondda declared that the decision lowered the status of all women. Undeterred, she had a lawyer draft the Parliament (Qualification of Peeresses) Bill to rectify the situation. Sponsored by two supportive MPs, the bill easily passed the Commons. The real battle came in the Lords, where Viscount Astor, Nancy Astor's husband, introduced it five times between 1924 and 1929. Women peers themselves expressed varying levels of interest but Rhondda recruited a few of them to lobby members of the Lords for the bill.

THE HOPE OF HER SIDE.

Above
Lady Rhondda goes out to bat for women at the House of Lords, *Daily Express* cartoon, 19 May 1922

In 1925 the bill was defeated by just two votes (78 to 80) and victory seemed near. But when it was presented again a year later its opponents rallied, filling the House with "backwoodsmen", hereditary peers who rarely attended, to vote against it. The bill was defeated by 126 to 80, an exceptionally high turnout for the time, showing how seriously members regarded the threat of female encroachment. In 1930 Astor tried to get the House to support the proposal in principle with a non-binding motion, rather than introducing the bill again. This was also rejected.

Some of the speeches in these debates were sexist and derisive. Fifteen women's groups protested against the tone of the 1926 debate. The opponents of admitting women to the Lords described the admission of women into the Commons, where Nancy Astor had ruffled sensibilities, as a mistake to be avoided. They challenged the qualifications of these "privileged ladies" to sit in the Lords (although simply inheriting a peerage was sufficient qualification for men). Birkenhead referred to women as mere "conduit pipes" for transmitting peerages between male generations, noting disapprovingly that some had not produced male heirs. Baroness Ravensdale, one of the interested women peers, likened the opponents of the bill to drowsy flies in a warm room, fearing the entry of a few hornets. Lord Astor responded to them by accusing his colleagues of treating the House like a golf club, where they could blackball applicants, rather than an assembly passing laws affecting 40 million people (including an increasing amount of legislation specifically concerning women).

The issue lay dormant until 1946 when the House considered proposals for the reform of the Lords which included the creation of life peerages and the appointment of new women peers. The suggestion aroused less hostility than before but consensus remained elusive. The proposals were withdrawn without a vote. Disappointed, Rhondda and Baroness Ravensdale consulted solicitor Edward Iwi, a constitutional expert, and with Baroness Beaumont they launched a petition in 1947 to demonstrate public support. Backers included the heads of women's colleges, veteran suffragists, bishops, cultural luminaries including novelist Rebecca West and actress Sybil Thorndike, and women's societies, which helped collect 50,000 signatures. At last in 1949 the Lords voted in principle to admit hereditary women peers. But the motion – introduced by the Marquess of Reading and backed by the veteran suffrage campaigner Frederick, now Lord, Pethick Lawrence – was not binding. While peers' attitudes had softened, the Labour government, committed to a more comprehensive reform of the Lords, stated, frustratingly, that extending the hereditary principle to women would be wrong, though some ministers were uneasy with this position. The Labour government was more concerned with the House of Lords' powers than its composition and passed the 1949 Parliament Act simply reducing its ability to delay legislation, despite MP Leah Manning's impassioned plea to include a clause admitting women as members.

By the 1950s most accepted that the House should include women – the situation appeared more absurd after Elizabeth II became Queen – but still disagreed over

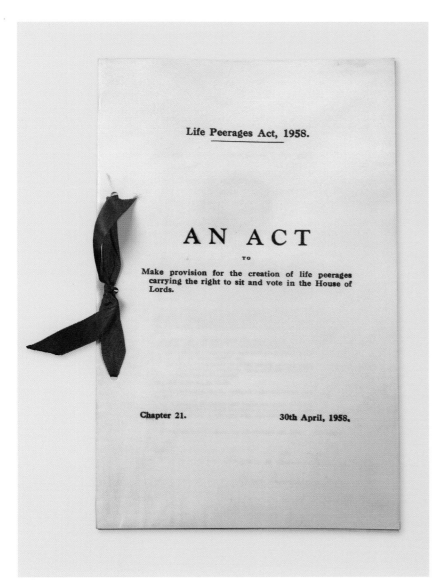

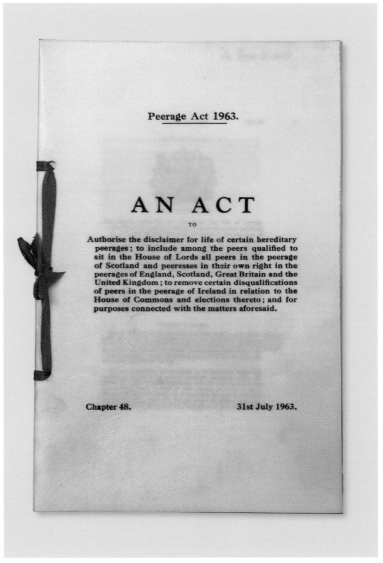

Above, left
Life Peerages Act 1958, the
Act that allowed women
and men to be appointed
Peers for life rather than
on a hereditary basis

Above, right
Peerage Act, 1963. This Act was passed
to allow Tony Benn MP to disclaim his
peerage. It also allowed hereditary women
peers to sit, therefore abolishing the final
inequality in Parliamentary membership

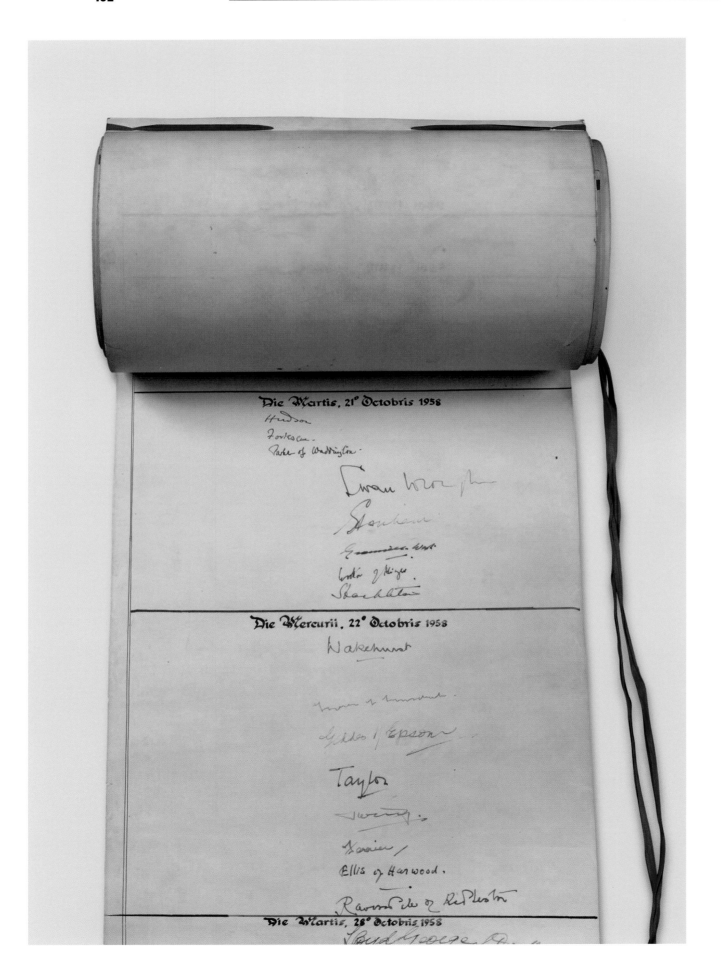

admitting them before more comprehensive reform. Ultimately it was the critical urgency of Lords reform which facilitated women's entry, though the intent was not to make it more representative but more effective. Its ability to legislate properly was crippled by an ageing membership, low attendance and serious party imbalance (Conservative hereditary peers greatly outnumbered Labour ones and Labour politicians were reluctant to accept hereditary peerages to close the gap). To recruit the new members required, the Conservative government finally adopted the idea of creating peerages that could not be inherited. The Life Peerages Act was passed in 1958. The Act ensured that women, as well as men, could become life peers, for it made no sense to continue barring half of the population if more members were needed.

A number of diehard peers continued to resist it. It was argued that the move could lead to the appointment of female ambassadors, which would be "vulgar", and that there was no room for the additional facilities that women would require; one even said that they did not want to sit with women on the benches or meet them in the library, candidly acknowledging that an underlying concern was maintaining male space. But these were now decidedly minority views. An amendment excluding women from the bill was decisively rejected. In the Commons, though, opposition to the bill came from the Labour party on the grounds that it would prevent proper reform. The Labour MP Jennie Lee unsuccessfully moved a similar amendment, unhappy with the idea that women peers might prop up what remained an undemocratic House of Lords. "The sooner it is replaced by a sensible and reformed House, the sooner we can get a decent improved constitutional arrangement," she argued. "If we cannot do that, if we have to have a second Chamber, let it be a sensible Chamber and, for goodness' sake, let us not try to drag in a number of women to camouflage it." She was opposed in the debate by Lady Tweedsmuir and Bessie Braddock.

The first 14 life peers included four women. They took their seats in October 1958, watched with interest by many women in the gallery. In common with the first women MPs, the majority had close family ties to Parliament. Three took no party affiliation. Katherine Elliot, Baroness Elliot of Harwood, was a Conservative party official, the widow of an MP, and a former United Nations delegate. Stella Isaacs, the dowager Marchioness of Reading, was recognised for having founded the Women's Royal Voluntary Services and became Baroness Swanborough. Irene Curzon, Baroness Ravensdale of Kedleston, a daughter of the staunch anti-suffragist Marquess Curzon of Kedleston, was nominated for her voluntary work, especially with youth clubs, and had been a hereditary peer since 1925. The only woman not following a male relation into parliament was social scientist Barbara, Baroness Wootton of Abinger, who "couldn't resist blitzing an all-male institution". A long-time magistrate and penal reform expert, she steered the bill abolishing capital punishment through the House in 1965 and became deputy speaker in 1967, three years before a woman attained this position in the Commons. The only discrimination she recalled was from the waitresses who suggested a women's table in the peers' dining room.

In early 1959 the Lords passed a further motion to admit the women hereditary peers but the government declined to act. They finally gained entry under the 1963 Peerage Act, which was primarily concerned with letting hereditary peers renounce their titles and stand for the Commons. The first to take her seat was Baroness Strange of Knokin, who had held her title since 1921. Some of those who entered the Lords, like Baroness Beaumont, had been waiting decades for admission. Viscountess Rhondda, though, was not among them, for she died in 1958, shortly after the first women life peers were announced. In 2011, she finally took her place in the House of Lords in another sense, when her portrait was hung in the peers' dining room to commemorate her campaign.

Opposite

House of Lords Test Roll, 1958. The Test Roll is signed by Peers as they take the oath. This Roll shows the signatures of the first four women to take their seats in October 1958

THE CHAMBER: 1963 AND AFTER

By 1963 women MPs had been elected for all major parties, and from all the constituent parts of the UK (Northern Ireland had its first female MP in Patricia Ford in 1953). A number of women had had a significant role in several parties. But women were still a tiny minority in the House of Commons, and there were no more than a handful in the Lords. It would take another 40 years before women occupied many of the most prominent political positions in Parliament and government – including the role of presiding officer in either House, symbolised by the Speaker's Chair in the Commons, and the Woolsack in the Lords.

Emma Crewe
Oonagh Gay
Emma Peplow

SELECTION COMMITTEES, QUOTAS AND WINNABLE SEATS, 1963–2015

There continued to be significant advances in the presence of women in the Commons. Women made a particular impact in the new and minor parties. In 1967 Winnie Ewing was only the second MP elected for the Scottish National Party (SNP). In 1969 the Irish Nationalist Bernadette Devlin made a strong impression as a 21 year old, elected for Mid-Ulster. Women who represented other minor parties include Caroline Lucas for the Greens and Naomi Long for the Alliance Party of Northern Ireland, both elected in 2010.

Diane Abbott's election in 1987 made her the first BAME (black, Asian or minority ethnic) female MP. Beatrice Wright had been the first woman to give birth as a serving MP in 1943, but the pregnancies of MPs Helene Hayman and Harriet Harman attracted much media attention in the 1970s and 1980s. As before, many women MPs had family connections with politics. Virginia Bottomley and Gwyneth Dunwoody were married to MPs at their first election. Harriet Harman's husband later became an MP. Winnie Ewing's daughter, Annabel Ewing, and daughter-in-law, Margaret Ewing, became MPs. The long-standing practice of widows taking over their husband's seat continued into the 2000s with Irene Adams and Gill Furniss.

Yet despite changes outside Westminster that increased female political activism and participation in the working world, it was not until the 1987 Parliament, when 41 female MPs were elected, that the proportion of women MPs in the Commons rose above five per cent of the whole House. It was clear the major obstacle to more women joining the Commons was the process of the selection of candidates by the political parties, and particularly selection by the major parties for "safe" or "winnable" seats. The percentage of female candidates had increased by 1992 to 18.3 per cent (up from 4.9 per

cent in 1945) but many of these women had little chance of topping the poll. Women in all major parties had difficulties in getting selected. MPs from both parties were questioned by selection committees about why they were leaving behind their husbands and families, or criticised for not knowing how to run a household if they were unmarried. Emma Nicholson was told by the Conservative Central Office that "the Conservative Party does not want women". Some Labour women felt excluded by the party's working-men's club, union-driven culture.

Things began to change in the Labour party in the late 1980s. Having avoided party politics in the 1970s, women's rights activists had joined the party in large numbers after Margaret Thatcher's election. Towards the end of the decade their interests aligned with a party leadership keen to modernise, especially after polling demonstrated that few female voters chose Labour. In 1983 the party committed itself to increasing women's involvement at all levels, and in subsequent years it adopted new rules designed to achieve it. In 1990 it set a target of women forming 40 per cent of Labour MPs by the year 2000. Shortly afterwards it introduced a policy of "all-women shortlists", designed to force local parties in half of the winnable seats to select women candidates. It was controversial amongst both men and women, and took the personal commitment of Labour leader John Smith to secure its passage. Challenged by two men who had been prevented from seeking selection by the policy, a tribunal decided in 1996 that the all-women shortlists were not lawful, ironically because of the Sex Discrimination Act 1975. By that time, though, enough women had already been selected to make a significant difference.

The number of women elected to the Commons had risen to 60 by 1992, but the biggest rise – to 120 – came as a result of Labour's all-women shortlists policy, at the general election of 1997. The increase had an immediate effect. One Liberal

Previous pages
Women Members of Parliament and former Members of
Parliament now in the House of Lords, by Rolf Marriott,
2015. On 18 March 2015, shortly before the House rose
for the General Election, all women MPs and former
MPs now sitting in the House of Lords, were invited to
sit for this photograph. The numbers they are holding is
their place in the order of all women ever elected to the
House of Commons – Constance Markievicz was No. 1

Below
Diane Abbott MP
photographed in June
2010, during her campaign
for the leadership of the
Labour Party

Democrat MP recalled in the History of Parliament's oral history project how exciting it was to be part of this "dramatic" change. A Labour MP already in Westminster noted how the appearance of the chamber changed suddenly with women standing out in bright, colourful outfits. There were extremely high expectations. Some feminists believed that there was now a critical mass of women at Westminster, who would be able to make real changes. More women began to be elected for the other parties as well. Conservative women were elected in much greater numbers after 2005; in 2015 SNP women made a breakthrough, with 21 elected, forming over one third of their parliamentary party. From all parties, women MPs formed 29 per cent of those elected in 2015, and their substantial presence in the Commons is now taken for granted.

WOMEN AND THE CULTURE OF PARLIAMENT

By the 1960s no one doubted that women should be involved in the political process. Yet it remained difficult for women to flourish in the overwhelmingly masculine culture and space of the Palace of Westminster. Interviews with women politicians, including for the History of Parliament's oral history project, testify to how much overt sexism remained in the 1960s and 1970s and even later. Women MPs were regularly mistaken for secretaries, employees or wives of MPs. It was frequently alleged that they were "more emotional" than their male counterparts. The Commons chamber, with its sometimes raucous, confrontational atmosphere, could be an intimidating place for outnumbered women MPs, whose sex could be used against them in personal attacks. For some it was worse: Barbara Castle wrote about a fellow cabinet member undoing

the buttons of her blouse during one vote, and more than one woman remembered being subject to groping within the chamber.

For most women politicians of this generation, this was part and parcel of working life. Many described having to "be tough" to succeed, or that it was "not as bad" as previous experiences in local government. Those who tried to change things found themselves facing more discrimination. Not all women sympathised with them, preferring instead to ignore the sexism and fit in with the men. Some rejected the idea that sexism was a problem at all, and argued that being a woman, and standing out from the men, could be a career advantage.

Westminster still had an atmosphere which many described as like a public school or a gentleman's club; women tended to refer to it more disparagingly as a "boys' club". Some women found it difficult to fit in. One, who remembered being welcomed by her male counterparts, still reflected that "men act in gangs" and "help other men out", excluding women from informal networks. Places like the Smoking Room were seen as not appropriate for women: one woman was told she was not a "nice girl" for venturing in. Yet to get things done, to keep up with the gossip and find out what was going on, women needed to enter these spaces and accept, ignore or counter the sexism they found there. Women also had problems with the press, which operated on very similar lines. Gendered press criticism, and a focus on dress, remained. Women seemed often to be "too" something – too colourful, too frumpy, too young or too old.

The timing and organisation of the Commons' sittings made things especially difficult for women with dependents, including young families. All-night or late-night sittings were common in the 1970s,

"The beastlier people are to me, the more sure I am of my own rightness. To go down fighting with no thought of humiliation or abdication, that's life's biggest thrill"

Barbara Castle

Right
Barbara Castle on the
House of Commons terrace,
photographed c. 1960

Above
Lady Olga Maitland,
photographed in July 1984

and the conventions of the House were not designed to accommodate children. Considered "strangers", children could not be brought into the chamber or voting lobby. The Labour MP Helene Hayman (now Baroness Hayman) became well-known when she had a baby in the difficult summer of 1976. A tiny Labour majority meant that all members were required to be on call in case a vote was called at any time while the House was sitting. Heavily pregnant, she was unable to leave the House on long, hot summer nights; back just two weeks after giving birth, she was forced to bring her son with her. The press covered her story in detail, and as a consequence she received plenty of hate mail accusing her of neglecting her child, though contrary to press reports she did not breastfeed in the chamber. She was far from unusual, although not all women had quite the same perspective. Some were without families; for some, with dependents far from Westminster, in their constituencies or elsewhere, the problem was a different one.

By the 1970s women from different parties were no longer sharing a room. Janet (now Baroness) Fookes described "real friendships" created in the Conservative room and Hayman the "solidarity"

of Labour's. However, it was now less common for women of different parties to mix or to work together. Some issues did provoke female collaboration: Conservative MP Marion Roe's breakthrough bill on female genital mutilation in 1985 required cross-party support. Nearly two decades later Labour's Ann Clwyd promoted the Female Genital Mutilation Act 2003, replacing the 1985 legislation.

Women often felt a responsibility to support campaigns on what were thought of as "women's issues". Jo Richardson promoted the Domestic Violence and Matrimonial Proceedings Act 1976 to give women who suffered from domestic violence the right to apply for an injunction. The Bill was taken up by the Labour government, as the first major law to recognise domestic violence as a crime. While Clare Short's attempts to ban *The Sun* newspaper's Page 3 photos of topless women were not successful, her campaign brought her much popular support, and *The Sun* eventually discontinued the feature. But those – for example pro-NATO defence campaigner Lady Olga Maitland – with an expertise on policy areas that were particularly dominated by men, often felt that they were shut out of these debates, though they campaigned on them regardless. And the range of subjects covered by women went well beyond "women's issues", working, for example, on private members' bills on very diverse topics. Dame Irene Ward secured several including the Rights of Entry (Gas and Electricity Boards) Act 1964, the Nurses (Amendment) Act 1961 and the Penalties for Drunkenness Act 1962. In 1960 Margaret Thatcher made her maiden speech introducing the Public Bodies (Admission to Meetings) Bill. Jill Knight piloted the Design Copyright Act 1968, a response to injustices suffered by a constituent whose work was subject to unauthorised copying.

From the late 1960s, women began to be appointed to more senior staff roles in Parliament. House of Commons Hansard employed its second permanent female reporter, Margaret Pass, in 1968; the following year saw Jacqy Beston (later Sharpe) and Alda Milner-Barry become the first women clerks since the Second World War. The House of Lords followed in the 1970s, with the first clerk, Fiona MacLeod (later Martin), arriving in 1981. Further breakthroughs came in the late 1990s with the arrival of the first "Lady Doorkeepers", Maureen Coxon in the Commons and Stella Devadason in the Lords. In 2008 Jill Pay became the first woman Serjeant-at-Arms, in charge of ceremony and security in the House of Commons. In 2018 Sarah Clarke was appointed the first female Black Rod (the counterpart of the Serjeant-at-Arms in the Commons). No women have advanced to the most senior positions of Clerk of the Parliaments or Clerk of the House.

WOMEN AT THE TOP

It continued to be rare for women to be ministers, and it took a long time for them to be accepted in more senior positions within the major political parties. But despite the obstacles, by the 1960s and the 1970s, a few women were taking positions of real standing and power within their respective parties. The careers of three of them, Barbara Castle, Shirley Williams and Margaret Thatcher – the most prominent and famous

Right
Jill Pay, Assistant Serjeant at Arms, by David Partner, 2007. Jill Pay was appointed Serjeant at Arms, the Parliamentary official responsible for security of the House of Commons, in 2008, the first woman to hold the post since its establishment in 1415

of women politicians in the 20th century – illustrate how gradually women advanced into the front rank of politics.

Barbara Castle was first elected as Labour MP for Blackburn in 1945. Her ability was recognised in the first Labour government formed under Harold Wilson in 1964, when she became Minister for Overseas Development, and then Minister for Transport in 1966. She was the first woman to hold successive posts in Cabinet. At Transport, she introduced major initiatives, including the compulsory wearing of seat belts and breathalyser tests. In 1970, as Secretary of State for Employment and Productivity, she was responsible for introducing the first equal pay legislation in 1970 and for an unsuccessful attempt to reform trade unions.

As Secretary of State for Social Services in 1974–6 she was responsible for a reform of state pensions to take account of years spent in caring responsibilities at home, and fought to introduce non-means-tested child benefit payable to the mother. After standing down from Parliament in 1979, Mrs Castle continued her career as a Member of the European Parliament and then in the House of Lords from 1990 until her death in 2002.

Shirley Williams, first elected for the Labour party in 1964, entered the Cabinet as Secretary of State for Prices and Consumer Protection in 1974. Her most important contribution, though, was to oversee the expansion of the comprehensive schools programme as Secretary of State for Education from 1976 to 1979. The move to abolish grammar schools and secondary moderns had begun under Margaret Thatcher in 1970, but Williams presided over a decisive but controversial change in British education policy. Defeated in the general election of 1979 and disturbed by the drift of Labour to the left, she resigned from the party and became one of the "Gang of Four", the founder members of the new Social Democratic Party (SDP). She became its first MP in 1981, when she won a by-election at Crosby, and was elected SDP President in 1983. But she lost her seat in the 1983 general election and never returned to the Commons. The SDP would merge in 1987 with the Liberals to form the Liberal Democrat Party. Appointed a Liberal Democrat peer in 1993, Williams served as that party's leader in the Lords from 2001 to 2004, retiring from the House in 2016.

Margaret Thatcher's achievement in becoming the first woman Leader of the Opposition and the first female Prime Minister was remarkable, given how few women had been Conservative MPs. She spent nearly a decade attempting to be elected as a Conservative candidate, finally winning Finchley in 1959. She was appointed Secretary of State for Education in 1970 in Edward Heath's administration, but she stood against Heath for the leadership of the Conservative party and won, becoming the Leader of the Opposition in 1975 – at a time when there were only seven Conservative women MPs in the Commons. She built on this success by leading her party to victory at the next general election in 1979.

Mrs Thatcher held the office of Prime Minister for longer than anyone else during the 20th century.

Below
Shirley Williams, photographed on her appointment as Minister for Home Affairs, 20 October 1969

Right
The Rt. Hon. Margaret
Thatcher OM, MP,
Prime Minister, by
Henry Mee, 1992

Above
**Virginia Bottomley,
Secretary of State for
National Heritage, at the
launch of International
Jazz Day, 1996**

Among the most influential of 20th-century prime ministers, she remains the most controversial. Her actions, for example, in instituting the right to buy for council tenants, going to war with Argentina over the Falkland Islands in 1982, and privatising major state-owned businesses – telecoms, gas, electricity and water – still arouse passionate support and hostility in equal measure. She lost office in 1990 when she was herself challenged successfully for leadership of the Conservative Party, after her poll tax policy proved unpopular with the electorate. Mrs Thatcher became a life peer in 1992. She died in 2013.

Mrs Thatcher did not include another woman within her Cabinet until Baroness Young became Leader of the Lords in 1982, and it was not until after John Major succeeded her as Prime Minister in 1990 that more than one woman sat in a Conservative Cabinet at a time – Virginia Bottomley and Gillian Shepherd were both in the Cabinet between 1992 and 1997. The Labour party briefly had a female leader in 1994, when Margaret Beckett became acting leader for a period after the sudden death of John Smith. Tony Blair's Cabinet in 1997 was the first to have as many as five women Cabinet Ministers at any one time. David Cameron's Cabinet had four in 2010, increasing to seven in 2015. In 2016 Theresa May became the second female Prime Minister, and

appointed eight women to the Cabinet, 35 per cent of its total membership. Since 2000, it has become normal for women to be senior ministers. They have held most of the major offices of state for the first time, including Home Secretary (Jacqui Smith, 2007), Foreign Secretary (Margaret Beckett, 2006), and Lord Chancellor (Liz Truss, 2016). The only exception remains the Chancellor of the Exchequer, a position which has never been held by a woman.

As women moved into positions of power within political parties, policy agendas began to change in response. The introduction of equal pay legislation in the 1970s is one example. The creation of a statutory minimum wage in 1998 was the biggest increase in women's pay since the Equal Pay Act 1975. Another example was domestic violence, although it was a backbencher, Jo Richardson, who piloted through the House of Commons the Domestic Violence and Matrimonial Proceedings Act 1976, the first major law to recognise domestic violence as a crime. More recently Theresa May, as Home Secretary in 2015, ensured that coercive control was included within the definition of domestic violence. Tessa Jowell, as Minister for Employment, was the prime mover behind the introduction of the right to request flexible working hours in the Employment Act 2002, and this right was eventually extended by

Above

Women Secretaries of State by John Ferguson, 2010. All served in the Labour governments of 1997–2010

the Coalition government to all employees in 2014. It was Harriet Harman, as Minister for Women and Equality, who piloted the Equality Act 2010 through the Commons, which harmonised and extended existing law affecting women's rights.

CHALLENGING WESTMINSTER CULTURE FROM THE 1990S

Many of the women who came into Parliament for the first time in 1992 and 1997 were from a younger generation, shocked to discover Parliament still dominated by a sexist culture that was increasingly challenged in wider British society. They described "boorish" and abusive behaviour in the chamber. Young women MPs were still mistaken for staff and secretaries, and it was still assumed that their interests would be limited to "women's issues"; some felt in addition that their growing numbers induced a stronger reaction from some men. Coverage of women MPs in the press and elsewhere continued to focus on their gender and their dress. Labour women who posed for an infamous photograph surrounding the new Prime Minister were labelled "Blair's babes". At the same time, they faced criticism from many in the women's movement for not doing more for women's interests. Analysis of their voting behaviour suggested that Labour women were less

likely to rebel against the party whip than were their male counterparts, though the reasons for this are complex. Some women argued that their style of politics was less confrontational, a more collaborative and behind-the-scenes approach, which was not respected by either the press or many in Westminster. Political scientists and historians remain divided about whether such a specific style exists, or how effective it was.

Nevertheless, the 1990s saw a shift in the attitudes, culture and working practices of Westminster, starting from the top. There had been women Deputy Speakers since Betty Harvie Anderson became the first in 1970, but it was not until the election of Betty Boothroyd as Speaker in 1992 that women started to significantly influence the working practices of the House of Commons. Boothroyd became an outstanding Speaker, commanding the confidence of the House at a time when John Major's government had only a tiny majority. She dispensed with the traditional wig, and introduced a more modern style of dress, and as such came to represent a new type of speakership.

Changing the way that the House of Commons was run, though, proved frustratingly difficult. The problems of doing so were symbolised by the demands to turn the rifle range into a crèche (the

"Elect me for what I am, and not for what I was born"

Betty Boothroyd, in the Speakership Election 1992

range survived until 2015). Even women could disagree on the nature of the changes required. The demand for "family-friendly" working hours for the Commons, for example, was of much less concern for those whose constituencies, and family homes, were well outside London, and who were unable to return to see children or partners on a free evening. Nevertheless, changes were made. Plans to modernise sitting hours had been under discussion since the early 1990s, but real progress was only made after 1997 and the establishment of the Modernisation Committee under the first woman Leader of the House of Commons, Ann Taylor. Under successive Leaders of the House, including Robin Cook, the committee became the driving force behind more "family-friendly" hours in the Commons. The time at which the House of Commons met was brought forward and time limits routinely placed on discussion on bills; the date of recesses was fixed in advance. Late-night votes and all-night sittings became much rarer, and the change fed through into changes in the culture of Parliament. Taylor had been one of the first women to become a whip, in the fraught Labour years of 1976-79, when the government's slim majority meant that every vote counted. In 1998 she became the first female Chief Whip, responsible for managing the Parliamentary Labour Party. There is some evidence that female appointments helped from the 1990s onwards to soften the traditionally aggressive approach of the whips' offices to ensuring the attendance of Members at key votes.

Women MPs began to chair select committees during the 1960s. Bessie Braddock was made chair of the Kitchen and Refreshment Rooms Select Committee in 1964/5, and Margaret Herbison chair of the Overseas Aid Select Committee in 1969/70. The establishment of the new departmental select committees in 1979 offered an alternative career to MPs. A number of women benefited, achieving prominence in the Commons and a considerable presence outside it. Renee Short was the first woman to take the chair of one of these committees (the Social Services Committee). Gwyneth Dunwoody was a formidable operator as chair of the Transport Committee, successfully defying the whips to keep her position when there was an attempt to remove her in 1992, a pivotal moment in developing the independence of the select committee system. Margaret Hodge was the first woman chair of the prestigious Public Accounts Committee in 2010. Reforms to the standing orders of the House to enhance the role of backbenchers, initiated in the wake of the disastrous expenses scandal in 2009, resulted in the creation of the Backbench Business Committee in 2010. The first chair was Natascha Engel, who was seen as effectively exploiting its powers for the benefit of the select committees and individual backbenchers.

From the viewpoint of the 2010s the House of Commons looks very different to what it did in 1963. The Conservatives and Liberal Democrats have both worked to address the lack of women in their cohorts. The SNP group elected in 2015 was 36 per cent female. A nursery was introduced in 2010, and a Women and Equalities Select Committee was established in 2015 to match the ministerial post created in 1997. The children of MPs are no longer

Right
The Rt. Hon. Betty
Boothroyd, by Andrew
Festing, 1994

Above
The Prime Minister and
Members from both Houses
gather in Central Lobby to
celebrate the centenary of the
Representation of the People
Act 1918, 6 February 2018

"strangers". It was the male half of Andrew Hames's Liberal Democrat parents, Duncan Hames and Jo Swinson, who first took him through the voting lobbies. Women MPs continue to work for a wide spectrum of policy issues through debates, questions, bills and amendments, and their achievements are no longer unusual or exceptional. Women MPs are now an essential component of today's Commons. But parity of representation remains some way off. The House of Commons has become considerably more female-friendly since 1963, but recent instances of harassment show that many inequalities persist, and it remains well short of perfect.

WOMEN IN THE HOUSE OF LORDS FROM 1963 TO THE PRESENT

The first woman to take her seat in the House of Lords, Baroness Swanborough, described the House of Lords as "a delicious place to be in. People move so slowly. Nobody runs down passages; nobody uses used envelopes; nobody does anything for himself if he can ask a gentleman with a gold chain to do it for him". Some male peers took time to adjust to the advent of women, with several complaining that women's lavatories took up space or even that women in politics was distasteful. But gradually women's presence was accepted, and women came to occupy an increasingly important role in the chamber.

As in the Commons, numbers of women in the Lords took a long time to grow to significant numbers. There was a small leap in the mid-1960s. As before, a number of the earlier appointments were wives or widows of senior politicians (for example Anna Gaitskell, Baroness Gaitskell; Barbara Brooke, Baroness Brooke of Ystradfellte; Clementine Churchill, Baroness Spencer-Churchill), although many of them had themselves been politically active, some of them – such as Violet Bonham-Carter, Baroness Asquith of Yarnbury – at the highest level. There were others who had themselves been MPs, such as Edith Summerskill (Baroness Summerskill), Frances Davidson (Baroness Northchurch), Irene Ward (Baroness Ward of North Tyneside), Alice Bacon (Baroness Bacon) and Jennie Lee (Baroness Lee of Asheridge) – despite the latter's opposition to the Life Peerages Act. There were some who had been important backroom political operators, women such as Beatrice Serota (Baroness Serota), quickly made a minister after her elevation to the peerage in 1967, or Marcia Williams (Baroness Falkender), Harold Wilson's political secretary who was accused of exercising an undue influence over nominations to the peerage in the so-called "Lavender list" affair of 1976. There were politically-associated campaigners, such as Betty Lockwood (Baroness Lockwood), equal pay campaigner and first chair of the Equal Opportunities Commission. But a growing number were less directly associated with party politics: Lucy Faithfull, Baroness Faithfull, elevated in 1975, was a children's campaigner; Sue Ryder, Baroness Ryder of Warsaw, who accepted her peerage in 1979, had become famous for her work on relieving post-war destitution in Europe.

By the early 1980s, women constituted a little more than 5 per cent of the House. As in the Commons, it was not until the 1990s, and especially after 1997, that there was a significant change in the proportion of women, though this was as much the effect of the removal of men as the introduction of more women: the 1999 House of Lords Act evicted all but 92 hereditary peers, thereby almost doubling the proportion of women peers from 8.8 to 15.8 per cent.

Allowing a relatively small number of hereditaries to remain was a compromise reached during the passage of the Act. The 92 were chosen by election by all of the hereditary peers. During the election, women secured the most votes in two of the categories in which the vote was organised: the Countess of Mar as a Deputy Speaker and Baroness Darcy de Knayth as a Crossbencher.

Following the removal of most of the hereditary peers, the independent House of Lords Appointments Commission was established in 2000 to appoint each year a small number of non-party political or crossbench life peers. Only 23, or 36 per cent of the life peers appointed on its recommendation by 2015 were women. Attracting applications from women, rather than the selection process, seems to be the reason for this low proportion: 80 per cent of the nominations the commission received in its first round were from men. The Appointments Commission's members have said that the calibre of those women candidates who were nominated was exceptional.

Most peers still, though, are appointed as a result of nominations by the leaders of the political parties. These appointments have been even more skewed towards men: only 22 per cent of those chosen by party leaders since 1958 have been women. Party peerages continue commonly to be a reward for service in the House of Commons (one quarter of

peers appointed between 1997-2015 were former MPs), so this poor record partly reflects male dominance in the lower house.

By the summer of 2017, nearly 26 per cent of the members of the House of Lords were women. Three groups have endured as overwhelming male: hereditary peers, bishops and law lords. Of the hereditary peers, only one is a woman and since the vast majority of hereditary peerages can only be inherited by men, few of the 92 are likely to be women in the near future. The 26 seats occupied by the Bishops were all taken by men until 2015 when the Bishop of Gloucester, Rachel Treweek, sat as the first woman Bishop. Only one woman – Baroness Hale – had been one of the Law Lords, who were members of the House of Lords and operated as the final court of appeal in the legal system, before the creation of the Supreme Court in 2009 and their removal from the Lords.

Although there have been far fewer women than men in the Lords, the women have had a disproportionate impact. One reason is that they attend more often. In the 1980s 44 per cent of women as against 22 per cent of men attended half or more of the possible sitting days. With the departure of most hereditary peers, many of whom attended rarely, the difference decreased, but was still noticeable. In 2010-2014 women peers

Left
Leaders of the House of Lords: Baroness Ashton of Upholland, Baroness Amos & Baroness Jay of Paddington, by Desirée Pfeiffer, 2008

Above
Baroness Hayman,
The Lord Speaker, by
Desirée Pfeiffer, 2008

attended 70 per cent of possible sitting days while men attended only 60 per cent. Women also relatively quickly took leading roles. The Labour peer Baroness Llewellyn Davies of Hastoe was the government Chief Whip in the Lords in 1974-9; Baroness Hylton-Foster was Convenor of the Crossbench peers from 1974 to 1995; and Baroness Young was Leader of the House from 1981 to 1983. This was far earlier than similar roles had been taken by women in the Commons. The first Lord Speaker, elected in 2006 following the separation of the roles of Lord Chancellor and speaker of the House of Lords, was Baroness Hayman (Helene Hayman); the second, who followed her in 2011, was Baroness D'Souza (Frances D'Souza). Six out of the last nine Leaders of the House have been women, one of whom, Baroness Amos, was also the first black woman cabinet minister in the UK.

Women peers are currently better represented on the front-bench in the Lords than are women MPs in the Commons. In 2015 only 24 per cent of ministers in the Commons were women, compared to 37 per cent in the Lords, and both Leaders of the House of Lords were women. The first Lord Speaker, Baroness Hayman, commented that "it gives me some quiet satisfaction that, should a man break through the glass ceiling to succeed me, he will be known as the first male Lord Speaker" (as Lord Foster became in 2016).

Women thrive in the upper House. Nothing compels backbenchers to attend, aside from requests from the whips or peer pressure, so those with dependents or time-consuming responsibilities outside are less disadvantaged than in most organisations. In the Lords' debates wit,

Left
Debate – Human Fertilisation and
Embryology Bill: Lord MacKay of Clashfern,
Lord Jenkin of Roding, Lord Alton of
Liverpool, Baroness Tonge, Baroness Barker
and Baroness Deech, by Desirée Pfeiffer,
2008. Participants in the debates on the
bill pictured in the House of Lords library

self-deprecation and a light touch are prized above aggression. The self-regulated chamber, with no peer chairing debates, operates rather like a Quaker meeting, and this suits women well. It has been argued, though, that the self-regulation of its debates can work against women: when there is strong competition to speak the House makes a collective decision who will speak next, and that choice may be influenced by considerations related to gender. When women fail to impress as speakers sometimes it is explained by reference to their gender – they might be described as sounding as shrill as "fishwives", for example. Like the Commons, outside the chamber or committees, the Lords feels like a gentleman's club. In the corridors and bars women can feel excluded and demeaned by comments on their physical appearance or assumptions about how they operate. And different women in the Lords, and different groups of women, may have different perspectives According to estimates, there were only 20 female black and minority ethnic peers in 2016. Three lesbian peers only came out recently (the first was Conservative Baroness Stedman-Scott), a reminder that some groups of women remain especially under-represented or marginalised.

Women peers' relatively high standing partly emerges out of the relationship between the two Houses. The Lords plays a less powerful role in the British constitution than does the Commons. Its classic role is to review and revise the government's proposed bills, rather than the direct confrontation over them expected in the House of Commons. Some members of the Lords on the government side become ministers and speak for the government, but they usually have less status than their counterparts in the Commons. Those who rise to the top of the Commons reach positions of considerable power. In the Commons politics is carried out in a series of competitive and aggressive rituals, designed to communicate the strength of one's own side and the weakness of one's opponents. In less publicly visible sites – the House of Lords chamber, committees and meetings and MPs' constituency surgeries, as examples – where politics is less concerned with competition and aggression, women parliamentarians tend to excel.

As Lord Longford claimed in a debate in 1985, "there is no side of British life where women are quite so prominent and influential as in the House of Lords". In theory, at least, all peers are equal: peers are listened to with equal respect and the impression they make on each other depends on how they perform. One expresses a typical view: "Working peers are not considered inferior, even former senior ministers are not looked up to. Dukes do not get more respect. Each peer is judged by their contribution, so internally it is a meritocracy." With just over a quarter of peers being women – 218 out of 837 in 2017 – there is clearly still far to go. But as the numbers of women have steadily grown over the last half century or so, they have become one of its most valued and powerful elements.

EXHIBITION CATALOGUE

Voice and Vote: Women's Place in Parliament
A public exhibition celebrating 200 years of women and Parliament

27 June – 6 October 2018
Westminster Hall, Houses of Parliament

VENTILATOR

Ventilator audio recordings
Extracts from 18th & 19th century debates in the
House of Commons, researched by the History of
Parliament Trust. Recorded in the current House
of Commons chamber by MPs and former MPs in 2017.
Acoustically modelled by the "Listening to the
Commons" project, University of York, funded by
the Arts and Humanities Research Council

**Wit's Last Stake or The Cobling Voters
and Abject Canvassers**
By Thomas Rowlandson, 1784
Print on paper
Parliamentary Art Collection WOA 6799
Illustration p. 15

Sketch of Ventilator, House of Commons
By Frances Rickman, 1834
Pencil on paper
Parliamentary Art Collection WOA 26
Illustration pp. 8–9

The Ventilator, House of Commons
By Lady Georgiana Chatterton, 1821
Pencil and watercolour on paper
Loaned by National Trust
/Shakespeare Birthplace Trust DR759/2
Illustration p. 11

**Roof of St Stephens, Listening to the
Debates thro' the Ventilator**
By unknown artist, 1833
Watercolour on paper
Loaned by Westminster City Archives E133.2(5)
Illustration p. 10

**View of the Interior of the House
of Commons during the Sessions 1821–23**
By James Scott, 1836
Print on paper
Parliamentary Art Collection WOA 2359
Illustration p. 12

Peterloo Massacre
Unknown publisher, 1908
Printed postcard
Parliamentary Art Collection Curator's
Reference Collection
Illustration p. 30

**Medal celebrating Henry Hunt's
election as MP**
By unknown designer, 1830
Silver
Parliamentary Art Collection
WOA M0633
Illustration p. 30

**The Destruction of the Houses of Lords
and Commons by Fire on the 16th Oct 1834**
By William Heath, 1834
Colour lithograph
Parliamentary Art Collection WOA 58
Illustration p. 33

CAGE

A Corner in the Ladies' Gallery
By Harry Furniss, 1888
Pen and ink drawing
Parliamentary Archives
HC/LB/1/112/248
Illustration p. 40

A View of the Ladies' Gallery
By Harry Furniss, 1906
Pen and ink drawing
Parliamentary Art Collection WOA 7606
Not illustrated

Caroline Norton (1808–77)
By Frank Stone, c.1831–41
Brush and ink drawing
Parliamentary Art Collection WOA 7486
Illustration p. 43

**Petition circulated by the Women's Suffrage
Petition Committee, 1866**
Loaned by LSE Library CB-001
Illustration p. 46

**Petition from the Mistresses of
Dulwich High School, 1884**
Parliamentary Archives HL/PO/6/11A
Illustration p. 51

Inaugural NUWSS meeting minutes, 1897
Loaned by LSE Library 2NWS/C/1
Not illustrated

Notice of formation of the NUWSS, Nov 1897
Loaned by LSE Library 2NWS/A/2/1/2
Illustration p. 60

The NUWSS "Tree", 1913
Loaned by LSE Library NUWSS leaflets to 1914
Illustration p. 75

The Women's Suffrage Pilgrimage, July 1913
Loaned by LSE Library 10/54/097
Illustration p. 74

NUWSS lapel pin
Parliamentary Art Collection WOA S750
Illustration p. 60

NUWSS pin badge
Parliamentary Art Collection WOA S745
Illustration p. 74

**National League for Opposing
Woman Suffrage badge**
Unknown manufacturer, c.1914–15
Parliamentary Art Collection WOA S749
Illustration p. 73

Wooden Suffragette Doll, c. 1912–14
On loan from a Private Collection
Illustration p. 73

Anti-suffrage postcards, c. 1912–14
Parliamentary Art Collection Curator's
Reference Collection
Not illustrated

Keir Hardie (1856–1915)
By Cosmo Rowe, c.1907
Lithograph with original pencil and ink signatures
Parliamentary Art Collection WOA 3645
Illustration p. 63

Interior of the House of Commons, 1850
By E. Chavanne, 1850
Coloured engraving
Parliamentary Art Collection WOA 1643
Not illustrated

Ladies' Gallery, House of Commons, 1870
Unknown artist, published by Illustrated London News
Print on paper
Parliamentary Art Collection WOA 6786
Illustration pp. 34–5

Cage audio recordings
Extracts from 19th and 20th century debates
in the House of Commons, researched by
the History of Parliament Trust
Recorded by actors for the Voice and Vote
exhibition in 2018

Eight chairs with red leather seats
Oak and leather
Parliamentary Historic Furniture and Decorative
Arts Collection
POW 00926, POW 00927, POW 01046,
POW 03735, POW 06724, POW 07040,
POW 07041 & POW 07052
Not illustrated

Proclamation Banner, 28 October 1908
Parliamentary Archives HC/SA/SJ/3/1
Illustration p. 67

Grille
Designed by AWN Pugin c.1850
Brass
Architectural Fabric Collection, Houses of Parliament
Not illustrated

Belt and chain, c.1840
Hiatt and Co Ltd, Birmingham
On loan from the Museum of London 61.186
Illustration p. 68

Porter's "Easy" Bolt Clippers No 2, c.1908–9
H K Porters, Boston, USA
Illustration p. 68

Police report referring to bolt clippers, 27 April 1909
Parliamentary Archives HC/SA/SJ/10/12/18
Not illustrated

Note on the purchase of bolt clippers, 10 July 1931
Parliamentary Archives HC/SA/SJ/10/12/67
Not illustrated

"A Great Orator" (H H Asquith)
By XIT Published in Vanity Fair magazine 1910
Lithograph
Parliamentary Art Collection WOA 6971
Illustration p. 62

Emmeline Pankhurst
By John H F Bacon c.1908
Chalk on paper
Parliamentary Art Collection WOA 5438
Illustration p. 59

Women's Suffrage (Miss Christabel Pankhurst)
By "Spy" (Sir Leslie Ward) Published
in Vanity Fair magazine 1910
Lithograph
Parliamentary Art Collection WOA 7608
Not illustrated

**Police report and press cutting
on Marion Wallace-Dunlop, June 1909**
Parliamentary Archives HC/SA/SJ/10/12/21
Illustration p. 75

**Fragment of broken glass from
Westminster Palace Hotel, 1911**
On loan from the Museum of London 60.166/1
Not illustrated

**WSPU Hunger Strike medal awarded
to Caroline Lowder Downing, 1912**
Silver and silk
The reverse reads, "Fed by Force 1/3/12 Caroline Lowder
Downing".
Parliamentary Art Collection WOA S748
Not illustrated

**Prisoners (Temporary Discharge for Ill-Health)
Act, 1913**
Parliamentary Archives HL/PO/PU/1/1913/3&4G5c4
Illustration p. 72

The "Rush", four postcards, 1908
Published by Sandle Brothers, London
Parliamentary Art Collection Curator's
Reference Collection
Illustration p. 65

WSPU Holloway Prison Medal, 1908
Silver and silk
Parliamentary Art Collection WOA M0564
Illustration p. 64

**Women's Social & Political Union
(WSPU) badge, c.1909**
Parliamentary Archives LCR/7/1
Not illustrated

Alice Hawkins' Illuminated Address
Print on paper
On loan from a Private Collection
Not illustrated

Alice Hawkins' scrapbook
On loan from family descendants of Alice Hawkins
Illustration pp. 70-1

Letter to Alice Hawkins from Emmeline Pankhurst, with WSPU envelope, 27 February 1912
On loan from a Private Collection
Illustration pp. 70-1

Selection of postcards from Alice Hawkins' collection, early 20th century
On loan from a Private Collection
Illustration pp. 70-1

Alice Hawkins' WSPU sash, c.1908
On loan from a Private Collection
Illustration pp. 70-1

Alice Hawkins' Deputation Badge, 1910
Satin and metal
On loan from a Private Collection
Illustration pp. 70-1

Alice Hawkins' Holloway Brooch, unknown date
Silver and enamel
On loan from a Private Collection
Illustration pp. 70-1

Letter to Alice Hawkins from M. Hulse, Her Majesty's Prison Leicester, 18 August 1913
On loan from a Private Collection
Illustration pp. 70-1

WSPU Hunger Strike medal awarded to Alice Hawkins, 4 September 1909
Silver and silk
On loan from a Private Collection
Illustration pp. 70-1

Copy of Portrait of Countess Constance Markievicz by Boleslaw von Szankowski (1873-1953), 1901
From the Collection of the Dublin City
Gallery The Hugh Lane.
Permission to reproduce granted by the Estate
of Boleslaw von Szankowski
Loaned by the Houses of the Oireachtas
Not illustrated

Representation of the People Act, 1918
Parliamentary Archives HL/PO/PU/1/1918/7&8G5c64
Illustration p. 77

Parliament (Qualification of Women) Act, 1918
Parliamentary Archives HL/PO/PU/1/1918/8&9G5c47
Illustration p. 77

Equal Franchise Act, 1928
Parliamentary Archives HL/PO/PU/1/1928/18&19G5c12
Illustration p. 87

TOMB

Nancy Astor's "Parliamentary Suit" 1919
Wool cloth suit (jacket and skirt), silk blouse and matching hat
Loaned by Plymouth City Council (Museums Galleries Archives)
Not illustrated

Nancy, Viscountess Astor MP Plymouth 1919-45
Zsigmond Kisfaludi Strobl, 1933
Plaster
Parliamentary Art Collection WOA S221
Illustration p. 83

Sutton Division Parliamentary Election Card, 14 Dec 1918
Parliamentary Archives LCR/2/1
Illustration p. 84

Appointment of Mrs Le Cras as Counting Agent, Nov 1919
Parliamentary Archives LCR/2/2
Illustration p. 84

Admittance Card for the Counting of Votes, 28 Nov 1919
Parliamentary Archives LCR/2/3
Illustration p. 84

Letter of thanks from Astor to Le Cras, 15 Nov 1919
Parliamentary Archives LCR/1/2
Illustration p. 84

Press cutting on Astor's victory, Nov 1919
Parliamentary Archives LCR/6/3
Illustration p. 84

Astor's first election campaign leaflet, Nov 1919
Parliamentary Archives BRO/1
Illustration p. 85

Scrapbooks of Norah Runge, 1931-35
Parliamentary Archives RUN/1-2
Illustration p. 91

Armchair with low back, 1900
Oak and leather
Parliamentary Historic Furniture and Decorative Arts Collection
POW 04870
Not illustrated

Armchair with rectangular back
Oak and leather
Parliamentary Historic Furniture and Decorative Arts Collection
POW 04743
Not illustrated

Pedestal desk inset with brown leather
Mahogany and leather
Parliamentary Historic Furniture and Decorative Arts Collection
POW 05352
Not illustrated

Pedestal desk inset with red leather
Mahogany and leather
Parliamentary Historic Furniture and Decorative Arts Collection
POW 05566
Not illustrated

Chaise longue, 1936
Oak and textile
Parliamentary Historic Furniture and Decorative Arts Collection
POW 07948
Not illustrated

Pedestal desk inset with black leather
Mahogany and leather
Parliamentary Historic Furniture and Decorative Arts Collection
POW 10135
Not illustrated

Sofa
Oak and textile
Parliamentary Historic Furniture and Decorative Arts Collection
POW 10692
Not illustrated

Hanging Shelves, 1840s
Oak
Parliamentary Historic Furniture and Decorative Arts Collection
POW 05760
Not illustrated

Tomb audio recording
Extracts from a newspaper article by Ellen Wilkinson MP, 1928
Recorded by an actor for the Voice and Vote exhibition in 2018

The Herbison Papers, 1950s
Papers and artefacts belonging to Margaret "Peggy" Herbison MP.
Parliamentary Archives HER
Illustration p. 97

Life Peerages Act, 1958
Parliamentary Archives HL/PO/PU/1/1958/6&7Eliz2c21
Illustration p. 101

House of Lords Test Roll, 1958
Parliamentary Archives HL/PO/JO/8/135
Illustration p. 102

Peerage Act, 1963
Parliamentary Archives HL/PO/PU/1/1963/c48
Illustration p. 101

CHAMBER

Chamber audio recordings
Oral history recordings of women MPs, 1960-2010
Sourced from the History of Parliament Trust and the British Library

Chamber vox pops
Recordings of current women MPs
Recorded for the Voice and Vote exhibition in 2018

ILLUSTRATIONS

p. 90: Private collection

p. 91: Parliamentary Archives, RUN/1–2

p. 92: Popperfoto/Getty Images

p. 94: Parliamentary Art Collection WOA 2936,
     © The Artist's Estate

p. 95: Parliamentary Archives, PUD/15/2/1

p. 96: J. Wilds / Stringer/Getty Images

p. 97: Parliamentary Archives, HER

p. 98: Parliamentary Art Collection WOA 7177,
     © Copyright holder

p. 100: Strube/Daily Express/Express Syndication

p. 101 (Left): Parliamentary Archives,
     HL/PO/PU/1/1958/6&7Eliz2c21

p. 101: Parliamentary Archives, HL/PO/PU/1/1963/c48

p. 102: Parliamentary Archives, HL/PO/JO/8/135

CHAPTER FIVE

pp. 104–5: © Palace of Westminster

pp. 106–7: Photo by Peter Macdiarmid/Getty Images

p. 108 (top): Photo by Terry Fincher/Daily Express/
     Hulton Archive/Getty Images

p. 108: Potter/Getty Images

p. 111: Parliamentary Archives, PUD/14/130

p. 112: Photo by United News/Popperfoto
     /Getty Images

p. 113: ©Parliamentary Art Collection WOA 6664

p. 114: Parliamentary Archives ,PUD/F/3373

p. 115: ©Parliamentary Art Collection WOA 3634

p. 116: Photo by Howard Denner/Photoshot
     /Getty Images

p. 117: ©Parliamentary Art Collection WOA 7169

p. 119: ©Parliamentary Art Collection WOA 3845

pp. 120–1: © UK Parliament/Jessica Taylor

p. 122: ©Parliamentary Art Collection WOA 6909

p. 123: ©Parliamentary Art Collection WOA 6916

pp. 124–5: ©Parliamentary Art Collection WOA 6913

ACKNOWLEDGEMENTS

This book is a collaboration between The History of Parliament Trust, the Parliamentary Archives, the Parliamentary Art Collection and St James's House. The editors are particularly grateful for the help of colleagues in the Parliamentary Archives and Parliamentary Art Collection, and staff of the LSE Library, in providing images for the book.

The Parliamentary Art Collection is owned jointly by the House of Commons and the House of Lords. It is the national collection illustrating the history of parliament and British politics over the centuries. The Speaker's Advisory Committee on Works of Art and House of Lords Works of Art Panel pursue active acquisition policies. Current priorities include the commissioning of portraits of current and recent eminent parliamentarians and reflecting women's contribution to parliament, both pre and post 1918. To find out more about the Collection, visit www.parliament.uk/art.

The Parliamentary Archives provides innovative and expert information management, preservation, access and outreach services enabling anyone in the world to use Parliament's records, both now and in the future. It holds over 8 km of physical records dating back to 1497 and its digital repository is growing rapidly. These records include many of the most important constitutional records in the UK, as well as four million others which have touched the lives of everyone and every community in this country and many abroad. To find out more about the Archives, visit www.parliament.uk/archives.

The History of Parliament is a research project creating a comprehensive account of parliamentary politics in England, then Britain, from their origins in the 13th century. Unparalleled in the comprehensiveness of its treatment, the History of Parliament is generally regarded as one of the most ambitious, authoritative and well-researched projects in British history. It consists of detailed studies of elections and electoral politics in each constituency, and of closely researched accounts of the lives of everyone who was elected to parliament in the period, together with surveys drawing out the themes and discoveries of the research and adding information on the operation of parliament as an institution. For more information about the History of Parliament, and to access over 20,000 articles on parliamentarians and constituencies, visit www.historyofparliamentonline.org.

CREDITS

St James's House
298 Regents Park Road
London N3 2SZ

+44 (0)020 8371 4000
publishing@stjamess.org
www.stjamess.org

Chief Executive
Richard Freed
richard.freed@stjamess.org

Managing Director
Stephen van der Merwe
stephen.vdm@stjamess.org

Sales Director
Richard Golbourne
r.golbourne@stjamess.org

Communications Director
Ben Duffy
ben.duffy@stjamess.org

Head of Editorial
Stephen Mitchell
stephen.mitchell@stjamess.org

Senior Designer
Aniela Gil
aniela.gil@stjamess.org

Deputy Editor
John Lewis
john.lewis@stjamess.org

INDEX